The Course

The Universal Path
Of Natural Life

by Hua-Ching Ni

SEVEN STAR
COMMUNICATIONS
Santa Monica, CA

SevenStar Communications Group, Inc.
1314 Second Street
Santa Monica, California 90401

Acknowledgments: Thanks to Suta Cahill, Janet DeCourtney, Arthur Sutherland, Michael Winn, and Lisa Zervakis for their assistance in editing and preparing this booklet.

First Printing September 1995

It is recommended that you study Hua-Ching Ni's other books and materials for further knowledge about a healthy lifestyle and to learn other practices. There are no claims for absolute effectiveness of the material in this booklet, which is to be used at your own discretion.

The College of Tao offers teachings about health, spirituality and the Integral Way based on the teachings of Hua-Ching Ni. To obtain information about the Integral Way of Life Correspondence Course, please write the College of Tao, PO Box 1222, El Prado, NM 87529 USA or call (310) 576-1902. To obtain information about Mentors teaching in your area or country, please write the Universal Society of the Integral Way, PO Box 28993, Atlanta, GA 30358-0993.

Library of Congress Cataloging in Publication Data
Ni, Hua-Ching.
    The power of positive living : the opportunity of a lifetime.
       p.   cm. -- (The course for total health)
    ISBN 0-937064-90-4
    1. Religious life--Taoism. I. Title. II. Series.
BL 1293.N545   1995   95-41898
299'.51444-dc20

Contents

Foreword

Tao, or the Way, is the natural unity of the universe. Human nature, when it is healthy, reflects that unity. When it deviates from this natural condition, confusion arises in the form of unhealthy social and cultural conditions. When this happens, the most dependable guide for returning to normalcy is the cultivation of unity in all aspects of one's life.

For many decades, I have promoted natural unity as my essential spiritual service. I hope that this book can demonstrate the direction of many generations of effort that have contributed to the truthful development of human life.

I intend to describe the efforts and achievements of the ancient developed ones in a concise manner that will hopefully shed light on the accomplishment of human beings who were committed to their own spiritual development and to the spiritual development of the world. My other publications present more detailed teachings of the Universal Integral Way of Natural Life, but this booklet outlines my teaching as a whole. Most of its contents were given to my friends at the "Taking Steps on the Thousand Mile Journey" retreat held October 28-30, 1994.

Introduction to
The Course for Total Health

I

Life is the convergence of natural energy.
Through evolution, it finds progress.

The spiritual path is not an external path. It is the path of
continually developing life. The subjective effort for a better
life is instinctive to most people, causing their latent self-
consciousness to be expressed in external pursuits. The
ancient culture of China expressed this human effort in a
natural way that is unique among all other cultures and
religions in that its central focus was immortal life. Ancient
sages discovered that spiritual energy, which is internal
energy, is the source of health and of a long and happy life,
when suitably strengthened and expressed.

The purpose of this series is to introduce this great body
of knowledge to you. Since it is not organized as a religion,
its pragmatic value in your life is your health. People live to
increase their health, and in turn their health serves their
happiness. This is the most conspicuous illustration of the
law of causality. The effect of doing right is to reward our
life and by doing wrong we punish ourselves. This is a
direct correlation that all people must face; no one can
evade it.

These teachings can serve you throughout your life.
They are the fruit of millions of years of attainment by
people whose long lives received the natural support of
their immortal souls.

II

The basic motive of life is to find happiness, and health is an
important part of that happiness. How, then, do you improve your health? Take more pills, go to more doctors,
spend more time at the spa? Ancient people did not have
such resources, yet records clearly show that there were

individuals who lived to be over a hundred years old and who experienced a state of health so complete that their strength and ability were considered supernatural.

In the *Course for Total Health* series, I will show you how health is related to more than just your physical body. Your health is affected, more than you may realize, by your mental and cultural attitudes, by your religious upbringing, and by environmental influences, including that of the society in which you live.

"No," many of you may be thinking, "my problem is that I need more vitamins or antibiotics." I do not wish to stop you from consulting your physician, but please read these booklets to get at the root of what can help bring you total happiness, health, well-being and success. Vitamins alone cannot bring happiness or health. Health comes from strong internal energy, which can also be called spiritual energy. People in ancient China worked to strengthen their spiritual energy in order to improve their lives and their health in totally natural ways. My work in the *Course for Total Health* is to introduce their great knowledge to you.

III

The first volume in this series, *Self-Reliance and Constructive Change*, discusses how being attached to cultural and religious fashions can hinder personal health and how you can go about detaching yourself from their influence.

The second volume, *The Power of Positive Living*, offers new ideas about simple improvements that can be made in everyday life to increase your positive energy and thus your health.

The third volume, *The Universal Path of Natural Life*, gives you simple guidelines for a natural, healthy personality, which is so rarely seen in these confused modern times.

The fourth volume, *The Natural Course of Spiritual Life: the Law of Causality*, is about changing your behavior and thoughts in order to create positive effects in your life to a degree you would never have thought possible. This includes health, wealth, happiness, better relationships, etc.

The fifth volume, *The Inner Source of Creative Life*, is a dialogue between myself and students who understand that health is not only skin deep and who ask questions about how to best focus their energies to improve their lives.

The sixth volume, *The Universal Mind*, discusses the connection between your conscious mind and the creative, empowering force that runs the universe: the universal mind. Increasing and enhancing this connection will awaken the power of healthy creativity within you.

The seventh volume, *The Universal Divine One*, contains the key to spiritual health and explains how uniting your life spirit with the divine spirit will elevate your life to a higher potential.

There will be more to come!

Introduction to
The Universal Path of Natural Life

(Adapted from Master Ni's statement of inauguration, February 4, 1978, Malibu, California.)

The Union of Tao and Man dates back to pre-historic China, long before China was known as a nation. At that time, over 5,000 years ago, there were no written languages, no nations and no royal courts. All human beings were equal manifestations of nature, and this tradition, as a manifestation of nature, did not belong to any nation or culture, only to great nature itself.

All Humankind Came From One Source
Humankind emerged as the manifestation of the combined energies of the sun, moon, earth and stars. Through the unification of these energies, humankind had the opportunity to take form as a wonderful being in this universe. It could also be said that the first humans came into being through the union of universal, creative *yang* energy and universal, receptive *yin* energy.

Our first ancestors are said to have originated in the yellow earth highlands of Asia, near the source of the Yellow River. Their progeny then scattered throughout the earth, combining their energies with those of new environments, adapting to their new surroundings and evolving a wide variety of physical appearances. Those who remained in that original locale are among the most ancient and pristine of all human beings.

Going back still further, however, all people have a common source of life in mother nature. The humanistic culture that was founded by Fu Shi, Shen Nung and the Yellow Emperor had one guideline: "All people are brothers and sisters." Recognizing the oneness of humanity is the true way to achieve universal harmony, which can also be called Tao.

Natural Spiritual Development

Human beings were born into this world with independent spirits and an integral nature and were originally endowed with great spiritual and physical abilities. They made less use of their minds than do modern people. It was through living in the world that people's minds developed a dualistic function that eventually dwarfed their original physical and spiritual powers. The mental perception of a perceiver that was separated from the perceived, thus mentally destroyed their connection with universal oneness. As the mind continued to develop, people's spiritual and physical faculties withered until they diminished themselves in body and segmented and disintegrated themselves in spirit. This also resulted in a shortened life span, from hundreds of years to a few decades. This is how humankind lost its natural completeness, independence and well-being.

In an attempt to remedy the problem, people eventually came to seek the truth through spiritual teachings or religions, not realizing that the true path to spiritual integrity lies within, and that the Tao is inherent in one's own nature. The purpose of the Union of Tao and Man, now the Universal Society of the Integral Way, is to be a lifeboat that enables an individual to eliminate all duality and separation and reunite himself with his true nature and actualize complete harmony with the eternal truth, the Tao.

According to the ancient teaching of Tao, the word "Emperor" meant a being who possesses and enjoys spiritual independence and completeness. Once you restore this spiritual independence within yourself, you restore your own natural and supernatural qualities as a universal sovereign. This is not just a myth. Rather than accept these words at face value, you can prove their truth for yourself. Spiritual independence is the reward of spiritual self-cultivation.

Nobody is born fully achieved. Development comes through the experience of living in the relative and dualistic world. Although people's experience of life may be the same, they are differently influenced by their natural environments and cultures, thus their levels of development are also different. Unsuitable development occurs as a result of emphasizing a certain partiality rather than balancing all three aspects of life as parts of a whole. As the human population has expanded, its spiritual quality has degenerated because of the mental distortion caused by worldly life. People become selfish, foolish, ambitious and insane as they focus on external profits and unnecessary contests of strength that are motivated by vanity rather than real threats to survival.

This kind of behavior does not come from the true nature of human beings, but from the incomplete knowledge of contorted minds. For example, by the act of comparison, the human mind tends to imitate others rather than think for itself. This causes people to forsake their intrinsic spiritual ability. The worst thing is that such mental partiality creates an addiction to incomplete intellectual knowledge and causes one to neglect his own blindness. Mental self-entrapment cuts one off from the source of true knowledge and results in profound misery. Only the human spirit has the ability to know the whole.

Individual Development is the Spiritual Vessel
Most people believe in a religion or follow a spiritual tradition in hopes of becoming a higher spiritual being or achieving a certain spiritual goal. However, without a healthy mind, spiritual goals are motivated by psychological need and vanity rather than personal growth and spiritual development. Few people truly pay attention to their character and work to improve their psychological health.

Dear students and friends, don't let any so-called spiritual teacher, pastor, priest or so forth, twist your vision and fool you. To develop spiritually, you must first learn to balance yourself and then restore your original, independent spiritual position in the universe.

The Universal Integral Way

The teaching of Tao, especially my own tradition, has been welcomed in this country after generations of public silence. In 1976, when I was practicing Traditional Chinese Medicine in Taiwan, some American students came to my door hoping to learn acupuncture. They soon discovered that Chinese medicine is only one aspect of the Universal Way of life. In order to broaden their study, they invited me to come to the United States and expressed their enthusiasm and sincerity to be initiated in spiritual alliance with the Union of Tao and Man (now the Universal Society of the Integral Way), which was eventually established as an educational religious organization.

According to my heritage, I am a spiritual child of this tradition and my spiritual realm is as wide and profound as my spirit can reach. All of my students are emperors and empresses of their own lives. They are spiritually self-enlightened and independent universes whose lives are deeply rooted in the eternal Tao. I use this day to renew myself, according to this tradition, as the head of this divine family and as the Master of the Union of Tao and Man here in America.

As we near the end of the 20th century, technology has reached its peak and the old spiritual traditions have been bankrupted, having died as a consequence of the drastic changes in today's world. Without a living spirit, they are no longer the same as when their founders were strong and they expressed the hearts and minds of an age.

However, this is a new age, in which all spiritual traditions are exposed to the challenge of modern technological culture. Although many religious followers and seekers of truth have turned away from the old traditions, some people are becoming aware that even the most advanced technological developments are unable to solve all of humankind's troubles. This tradition firmly accepts the challenge. It is a super-science based on highly developed natural knowledge of the universe. It contains methods and practices that were developed and, more importantly, used by masters to help themselves and build spiritual heirs, some of whom are Mentors of the Universal Society. This tradition, which extends its teaching from generation to generation, will always be fresh and vital as long as there are people who feel that spirit itself is the essence of life.

I was spiritually crowned the day I achieved my enlightenment, being enthroned by the high energy and wisdom of my masters, who entrusted their development of many lifetimes to me as their spiritual heir. This inauguration is not for my personal glory, but rather the glorification of the human spirit. It is not a superficial ceremony. It is an occasion for illuminating the principles and teachings of this tradition in a new land.

Thank you for attending this ceremony. Developed ones always consider themselves as guests who have come to serve the world. Ordinary religions stretch out their vines like ornaments to cover mental darkness. This tradition, however, is firmly rooted in the enlightenment and truthful spiritual achievement of individuals.

Spiritual achievement always depends on one's own self-cultivation. I will not easily recognize anyone as an heir to this tradition unless true spiritual progress and achievement is apparent. This will guarantee that the spiritual qualities and standards that we respect will not fall due to social favor or corruption.

My shrine is just an ordinary house. In fact, this room is a remodeled garage. You may think it is a joke that a master inaugurates himself in the garage of an ordinary house. Perhaps if you were invited to the coronation of a queen or king you might feel more honored. However, please remember that the spiritual value of this inauguration is more lasting and far reaching than any social or political event.

It is a spiritual truth that miraculous things are usually disguised in ordinary clothes. Even if an achieved one were to sit here radiating sacred, spiritual energy to all of you, it would depend on the spiritual eyes of the participants to witness such heavenly sublimity. Your own spiritual quality is what makes this occasion more significant than any religious or political ceremony. What I share with you on this occasion is that wonders can take place even in the most commonplace surroundings. Tao exists everywhere, at every moment, and is now manifesting itself in the form of a man illuminating the minds of all who join him here, and even those who are not here today. I encourage everyone here to realize the value of their own life beyond all expressed form.

We now continue the timeless wisdom that began millions of years a go with the first human beings. It is my hope and wish that you will also be able to continue the independence and integrity of the human spirit for billions of years to come. Thank you.

NOTE: The original Union of Tao and Man, founded in 1976, gave birth to the Universal Society of the Integral Way in 1993. The spiritual heirs of this tradition are the Mentors and members of the USIW. Mentors are certified yearly by the USIW and accept a unified discipline as their moral foundation. They can withdraw from the society whenever they feel the need to adjust themselves. The USIW was organized by Mentors who have dedicated themselves to promoting Master Ni's teaching worldwide.

Chapter 1
General Information
About the Teaching of Long, Happy Life

1. Name: The Way or Tao is known by scholars as a philosophy, while to general Chinese society, Tao is known as the ancient way to live a long happy life. To serious followers, it is known as the Universal Integral Way.

2. The Nature of the Teaching: Although I use the word "teaching" to describe the Way, it is actually a model of living, not just a teaching in the sense of a school or religion. Its teaching is that of natural life, which contains the possibility and potential for higher development. Please bear this in mind as you read this booklet. The Way is not an artificial faith, nor does it glorify anyone or anything, rather it strengthens your own natural confidence so that you can attain a long and happy life. It is transreligious, and thus is universal. It does not call part of its nature God and another part the devil. It is not about warrior worship, nor does it say that God will take your side in a war or always forgive you if you constantly make trouble for yourself and others. It teaches humans to become self-reliant and develop a universal conscience.

As the natural oneness of universal life, Tao is above all religions. As a teaching, it reveals that happiness is something you achieve for yourself, and that trouble and punishment are invited by your own ignorance and carelessness. Spiritually, you are totally responsible for your own life.

3. The founders of this teaching were people who developed themselves naturally. Some of them who are still remembered by name were:
Kwan Tsen Tsu
Tien Tsing Wan Ren

Yung Tsen Kung, an early teacher of sexual health
Che Po, a teacher of natural medicine and one of the early
acupuncturists
Rei Kung, an herbalist
The Lady of the High Heaven, a divine being
Fung Hau, a military strategist

These were the teachers from whom Yellow Emperor collected knowledge and practices. The Yellow Emperor, who
reigned from 2698 to 2598 B.C.E., was a cultural and
spiritual leader of ancient China. This tradition respects him,
not because he was emperor but as a model of a complete
life. He did not give up society for the sake of his own
spiritual achievement, but devoted his life to help the
troubled world by developing written language and cloth-
ing. He also invented the compass and forbid people to
burn the mountain forests. He improved agriculture and did
many other good things too numerous to describe.

4. The Earliest Followers:
The family and followers of the Yellow Emperor
The people of the Yellow Emperor's time

5. The Early Promoters:
The scholars and teachers of the Chou Dynasty, 1122-249
B.C.E., promoted the natural lifestyle and philosophy of
early human history from the time of the Yellow Emperor.
    After the Shah Dynasty (2207-1767 B.C.E.) and through
the Sharng Dynasty (1766-1121 B.C.E.) people become
overly religious. A system of voluntary slavery appeared and
society became dependent upon religious leaders. These
leaders' decisions depended on the size of donations that
people gave them. There was serious corruption in such a
society.

By the end of the Chou Dynasty (1122-249 B.C.E.), society was morally corrupt. Great confusion began in the weakened centers of the warring feudal states. People became discontent with the simple nature and honest ways. Thus, teachers arose during this period, and established the Golden Age of Chinese culture.

6. The Most Well Known Teachers:
Yellow Emperor
Lao Tzu
Lieh Tzu
Chuang Tzu
There were many others who lived peaceful lives of personal spiritual development and left no trace of their lives.

7. Books and Records
The Yellow Emperor's *Nei Ching* (Internal Work)
The Yellow Emperor's *Four Books*. This book was used as a
    political manual in the early Han Dynasty (206 B.C.E.-
    209 C.E.).
The teachings of Mo Tzu, Lao Tzu, Confucius, Menfucius, Chuang Tzu and all important classics of the ancients which were produced or collected during this period.

8. Early Development Influenced by the Yellow Emperor:
Medical schools
Art of the Inner Room (natural healthy sexual instruction)
School of Immortality (a special knowledge and practice)
School of Tao (the Way)
School of *Yin* and *Yang* (natural and climatic energy)
School of Legend Study (oral history and spiritual metaphors)
School of Military Strategy
School of Astronomy
School of the Five Element System
Dream Analysis

Groups of scholars who studied, practiced, and used these arts formed different schools based on their specific knowledge and practices.

9. The Most Active Times:
Near the end of the Chou Dynasty (1122-249 B.C.E.)
After the fall of the tyrannical first Emperor of Chin (248-207 B.C.E.), the teaching of the Way was used to guide the restoration of a natural society.
The early Han Dynasty (206 B.C.E. - 219 C.E.), the teaching of the Way was used for political guidance.

10. Nature of the Teaching:
Special knowledge, attainment and practices were passed from individual to individual among followers, nature lovers, researchers, and those who engaged in spiritual self-cultivation. Many of these people also offered social service.

Because of its timeless connection to all people, the Way is the oldest trans-religious religion.

11. Relationship With the Later Religion Called Taoism
Although Tao is respected and exalted by Taoism, Taoism has no relationship with the Yellow Emperor's spiritual and cultural leadership or with natural spiritual civilization.

Exorcistic Taoism became active at the end of the Han Dynasty and caused the fall of the dynasty. Monastic Taoism became the new religion of the Yung Dynasty (1280-1367 C.E..). Both of these forms are still active, as are other types of religious Taoism.

12. The Ancient Achievement Was Preserved By:
Recluses
Ordinary people and professionals
Newer religious sects
The general culture of China

13. Modern Followers Include:
Scholars in China and abroad
My family, students and friends
Recluses
Newer religious sects
Ordinary people and professionals
Certain aspects of general Chinese culture

14. Modern Promotion:
The broad spiritual teaching of the Universal Integral Way
The Self-Reliance Health Program

Chapter 2
Respect the Natural Unity of All Things

The most developed, ancient wise ones respected the original essence of the universe. Universal oneness does not require any effort to achieve; it is innate and natural. It can be called Tao or the Way or the eternal universal flow, but on a human level it is the natural wisdom that maintains the spiritual unity of life and thus supports health and harmony.

Therefore, there are two types of human spirituality: religion and the direct pursuit of natural unity above all cultural or religious limitations.

Highly developed sages appreciated the unity that comes from maintaining a balance between objective and subjective conditions. True development is based on spiritual growth and natural life experience. Human religions define the indefinable power of universal unity behind all things in an attempt to establish permanent solutions to what is temporary by nature. Whenever people treat an interpretation of the truth as if it were eternal, they overlook the subtle truth and create trouble for themselves and others.

In Chinese, the term Tao indicates ancient spiritual efforts that have been variously interpreted by later religions, but the Way contains the hint to move forward not to stay. The goal of the ancient spiritual achieved ones was a natural life in pursuit of universal unity. By separating themselves from religious formalities, wise students come one step closer to the original simple essence behind all things: Tao.

Organized religions do not respect the natural unity within each individual or in nature itself. By establishing their own spiritual "realities," they transform minor individual conflicts into major social conflicts and replace the true divinity of universal oneness with shallow doctrines.

In the past 2,000 years, some spiritual individuals have tried to overcome the conflict between an external notion of divinity and the internal human reality. In Chan or Zen Buddhism there were quite a few masters who regained personal unity through direct experience. Likewise, Sufism has attempted to correct the suppression of internal natural spirituality by fundamentalist Islamic teachings in the Middle East. And in Western society, most Christians fail to see the truth that Jesus' teaching of internal unity was intended to correct the almost exclusively external faith of his society.

The teaching of Tao serves the world by helping quiet surface conflicts so that people can see the deep truth of their own natural being. Without unity, one's body, mind and spirit become buried by the trivia of life. When unity is found, a person has the same potential as any sage who ever lived.

Chapter 3
The I Ching

An ancient paradigm of the universe is presented in two cosmological diagrams called *Hu Tu* and *Lu Su* . In the West, this paradigm was known as the "magic square." These ancient mathematical symbols, which were developed over a period of 20,000 years, are discussed in my book *Mysticism* and *The Book of Changes and the Unchanging Truth* and in my upcoming books *The Reunion of Mind and Spirit*, and *The Paradigm of the Universe*. They are the basis of the *I Ching*, which is at the core of many useful cultural developments and represents the spiritual attainment of millions of years of human growth. The *I Ching* benefits the mind by guiding it to understand the relationship between itself and nature. It offers proof of the subtle connection between the sphere of self and the sphere of non-self. In modern terms, the *I Ching* is the ancient theory of natural universal evolution. The ancients' achieved vision allowed them to perceive the natural patterns of evolution. The *I Ching* also appears to have been the foundation of the ancient natural sciences.

Chapter 4
The Hidden Truth of Nature

There is a very short, condensed message of ancient wisdom called the *Yin Fu Ching*, which could be translated as "The Hidden Truth." It is recognized as a legacy of the Yellow Emperor, although it appeared during the Tang Dynasty. It is somewhat easier to understand than the *Tao Teh Ching*.

This classic was passed down from the great old fisherman, Chiang Shan, who assisted the rise of the Chou Dynasty. This piece and "The Instruction of the Respectful Yellow Stone" (which has been printed in *Progress Along the Way: Life, Service and Realization*) are spiritual gems from the tradition of the Universal Way of Integral Truth.

I believe the *Yin Fu Ching* was written before "The Instruction of the Respectful Yellow Stone" and the *Tao Teh Ching*. Although the original Chinese text is simple and short, one Chinese character can have many layers of meaning. Sometimes you read or understand it one way, and another time you can read or understand it a different way, according to the depth of your own understanding and experience. This ancient piece is divided into three sections called the Upper, Middle and Lower Spheres. It contains what I would call "the bottom line" of nature's truth.

The Upper Sphere
Observing nature
    and controlling one's relationship with nature
    is the way to achieve a good life.
In nature, there are five bandits.
Only the one who sees them can live a better life
    by balancing his life.

The five bandits are:

9

1. *Nature makes you desire to be born.*
2. *Nature makes you desire to live.*
3. *Nature makes you desire to eat.*
4. *Nature makes you desire to have sex.*
5. *Nature makes you disappear from*
      the apparent sphere of life.

The five bandits come from within life,
      because nature is performing its will through you.
It is nature that employs your hands to create things.
It is nature that employs your body to produce all things.
Nature transforms itself to become you and others.
It also endows you with a mind
      which becomes the authority of your life.
First recognize nature with your mind,
      then you will understand
      the position of life in nature.

When nature becomes destructive,
      the stars and the constellations
      are disordered in the sky.
When the earth becomes destructive,
      big disasters come like monsters upon the land
      and swallow lives.
When people become destructive,
      the natural order that sustains life is destroyed.
When nature, earth and people harmonize,
      there is balance and stability
      and a good life for all beings.

Among people, there are those who are clever
      and those who are clumsy.
Life is a matter of how people manage themselves
      and how they relate to nature and to one another.

The clever one may get himself killed.
The clumsy one may make himself better off.
It is a matter of knowing how to steer one's life
     and not violate the principle of harmony.

People have nine orifices that express different needs.
The nine orifices can get you in trouble.
The eyes, the ears and the mouth
     are the main culprits.
It is important to know
     whether it is suitable to move or to be still.
An improper move or an untimely act
     is just like fire;
     it is derived from wood,
     but it also destroys the wood.
An improper move is like treachery
     growing inside of a nation (an individual life);
     when the opportunity is right,
     the nation will be ruined.
Watch for trouble that comes from within,
     from living your life improperly.
The one who knows to prevent things
     from becoming destructive,
     both inside and outside,
     is truly wise.

The Middle Sphere

Nature gives birth to your life.
Nature also takes your life away.
This sounds reasonable.
Thus nature is the thief of all lives and things.
All things and all lives are the thieves of human life.
Human life is a thief of all other things and other lives.

When all three thieves balance themselves,
*   without any one of them being overly extended,*
*   there is great peace.*
When you eat at the right time,
*   it sustains your physical survival.*
When you make a correct move,
*   it is of benefit to all.*

People marvel at strange phenomenon as holy.
They don't notice the ordinary things
*   that are truly sacred.*

Days and months can be numbered.
Things big and small can be known.
This is the surface from which general knowledge comes
*   and the foundation of all creative work.*
Although the deep secret knowledge
*   reveals itself all the time and everywhere,*
*   people don't see it and don't know it.*
The virtuous one who attains such deep secret knowledge
*   enjoys peace.*
When the unvirtuous attain this knowledge,
*   they use it to live a fanciful life.*

The Lower Sphere
Blind people's ears are sharp.
Deaf people's eyes are sharp.
This is a matter of concentration.
When you are able to concentrate,
*   you are ten times more powerful than a whole army.*
If you can keep quiet for three days and three nights,
*   you can find your own solution to trouble.*
You are ten thousand times more powerful
*   than a whole army.*

Desire is stirred up by things.
Your desire dies after being satisfied with things.
Desire is most stirred by eye contact.

Nature has no mercy;
thus, it has great mercy on all.

Sudden thunder and strong wind are insensitive.
The one who possesses high joy
must be stupid.
The one who becomes very quiet
must have a nature which is clear and clean.

Nature is so selfish,
but its use is so public.
The goal of life is to control chi *(energy).*

Life is the root of death.
Death is the root of life.
Grace is begotten from harm.
Harm is begotten from grace.

Foolish people treat heaven, earth, politics,
economy, religion and logic as holy.
I treat right timing, right action and good ideas ,
with right communication and application,
as the most supportive things in life.
People admire sages but remain foolish themselves.
I don't endanger my life by my own foolishness.
Vulgar cultures and leaders
value excellence or unusualness
in things and people.

I think that unusualness or excellence
    have no supremacy.

People risk their lives
    to drown in water or to walk through fire.
That is a way to risk their own lives.

The way of nature is quiet and inactive,
    it is permissive and grants freedom to all.
Thus, all lives and all things take form by themselves.
The way of nature is pervasive.
Thus, yin and yang interact,
    embracing and assisting each other.
Through the harmony of yin and yang,
    all changes and transformations occur smoothly.

Sages know that the way of nature cannot be violated.
Therefore, they become very quiet and peaceful.
When people come to be quiet and peaceful,
    even the influence of time
    and the wasteful commotion of society
    have nothing to do with them.
The one who has natural spiritual depth
    witnesses the birth of all phenomena.

The I Ching *is where the true secret*
    of nature is expounded.
It expresses how yin *and* yang *can balance each other.*
That is how to keep up with
    and live in harmony with universal nature.

This was not only an important teaching of its time, but contains spiritual guidance of perpetual value.

Chapter 5
The Development of Humankind and the Universe

It is a spiritual reality that the human soul evolves side by side with physical nature, because both the physical and the subtle spheres of the universe are manifestations of the subtle origin, which progresses through different stages of evolution. It can be said that universal nature and the human soul evolve through the same process and at the same pace.

The direction of universal evolution is upward, from the physical to the spiritual level. The human soul is a continuation of natural physical evolution in which the physical and spiritual spheres of life unite for the further evolution of universal divine oneness. This evolution is self-accomplished and is not subject to interference from any external god (i.e. projections of the human mind).

The subtle law is externally expressed as the process of evolution. In other words, the same light that guides a person to discover oneself internally also helps him or her discover the universe externally.

Chapter 6
Yin and Yang and God

Moving from left to right, up and down, expanding and contracting, etc. comes from the alternation of *yin* and *yang*. *Yang* has the sense of being positive, and *yin* the sense of being negative. Endless interplay between them occurs, until a stage of balance is reached.

The law of *yin* and *yang* also illustrates the principle that a thing turns into its opposite if pushed too far. This means that once a certain limit is reached, a swing in the opposite direction is inevitable.

In human life, God is the name for the unity of *yin* and *yang*, but they could also be called the rational fulcrum that reverses direction before an irreversible extreme is reached. For example, God is what can prevent divorce or violence from happening.

The Integral Way is the natural process of evolution. The human soul or self-assumed God was not the creator of the universe, because the universe does not need to be created, it is divine. It develops itself without needing to be told to do so. The human soul is a product of this natural self-evolution.

If no God existed prior to the conceptual human mind, then what exactly is God? God is the result of using self-awareness to recognize one's own spirit. There is no external authority, only the subtle connection among all souls known as the subtle law. The *Tao Teh Ching* clearly states that the Way precedes God, not that God precedes the Way.

As a result of development, the human soul and mind are able to serve as the fulcrum point of life, providing internal adjustments to opposing pulls of *yin* and *yang*.

God can also be understood as the unity of all spirits, the equipoise between the movement of *yin* and *yang*, yet God is also within *yin* and *yang*. It is the unity that holds together or connects all human souls, because it is all souls. Human souls evolved from it, and can become aware of it.

The conceptualization of God as an external being is a creation of the human mind. The childlike image of God as a superhuman judge is nothing but a heroic self-image. No God existed prior to nature itself.

God is the balance between nature and the subtle universal law of nature, not the mother or father of nature. You may wonder then, what did create nature? There never was a creator, in the sense of an individual being. Creation arose through the interplay of *yin* and *yang,* two seemingly opposing forces that accomplish each other. The universe started as chaos, but then chaos developed into an orderly world, according to the *yin-yang* principle.

The universe forms itself, operates itself, and sustains itself through the interactive relativity of *yin* to *yang* to *yin* to *yang,* endlessly revolving and evolving.

Chapter 7
Natural Facts of the Soul

The human soul is the result of natural biological evolution which moves forward by integrating spiritual elements from the sky with life's self-produced *hun* and *po*. The early stage of a human soul consists of a conscious mind and subconscious emotion, which is sometimes active in dreams, but a soul also contains the potential for higher development, such as conscience and rationality, which can be enhanced by education and spiritual development.

Given this plain natural reality, there is no need for salvation unless your soul becomes weakened by your own wrongdoing. Even then, religion still cannot save you. You must help yourself. Only spiritual self-cultivation can correct your mistakes and disperse the miasma of society, religion and culture, and of your own life experience. Even if you use the conceptual tools of religious belief, the understanding of how to use them comes from you as an individual, unless you have been brainwashed.

The home of your soul is your body. You don't need to haunt any church or temple. They are not true houses of the soul, they are mostly the houses of the lost. You may wonder what the destination of your soul is. Nature is orderly, and you have your place in the natural spiritual world. Once you dissolve the sense of self, all souls become one; you become the universal soul. This is why I ask you to respect the Universal Divine One, which includes not only souls with no physical form, but also those which are in the form of human life.

Suppose there is a soul that clearly remembers its life experiences from a different time. Such a soul is like a swimmer sitting alongside a stream. After swimming, he returns to the shore for the light and air. Each time he dives into the human world, he experiences that the world has become externally different, yet his soul still retains its spotless purity. He can undauntedly re-enter the rushing current without ever being discouraged. Is this soul a god? I think so, because of its indestructible quality. An undefeated spirit challenges death and enjoys the everlasting glory of universal life. This could be your soul or my soul. Its truth is reflected to you by the Universal Integral Way.

Many people may wonder whether their soul is immortal, since they cannot remember other lifetimes. In each rebirth, we are like new. No one is required to identify with the past. Even if you do not think your soul is immortal, the Universal Way is immortal. It was not less so in ancient times, it is not more so in modern times, it is the immortal truth of your immortal soul.

The soul itself is pure natural matter, and it needs healthy activity. This is why I have written so many books, to provide good spiritual nutrition that will enable you to attain the Universal Way of Integral Truth.

Chapter 8
Evolution

The process of human spiritual growth is a reflection of one's external life activity. There is no need to go to school to learn this process, because it happens naturally, from life experience, if an individual follows the inner teacher of his or her own nature.

All evolution starts in darkness, including the brightness of human civilization. The evolution of the human soul is part of the evolution of nature. Humans were formed millions of years ago from within that darkness. The Mother of the Universe conceived us and the world from the reproductive energy of nature and formed us in the shape of human life in her womb. The soul and the mind developed slowly and naturally, not through any teaching or separate divine plan.

Through the process of evolution, three things can be known: the indestructibility of matter, the indestructibility of the soul, and the indestructibility of the personality. In other words, evolution exhibits the law of conservation of matter, the law of conservation of soul, and the law of conservation of personality. On the surface, all people and all matter are destructible, but at a deeper level, energy cannot be created or destroyed; it only changes form through its internal structure and external shape.

Internal spiritual evolution is what reforms the soul to become better and stronger. Your personality is your spiritual form expressed in real life. Your spiritual character is formed by different spiritual qualities. Through spiritual self-cultivation, we can refine ourselves to have the same qualities as achieved ones such as Jesus, Sakyamuni, Lao Tzu and others who developed a high sense of responsibility and commitment to all lives. They are human gods whose individual life expressions may be different, but whose purpose is the same.

Matter is indestructible. Natural material, at its base, is the best, because its transformation is not disturbed.

The human soul, at its base, is indestructible. A natural soul is the best, because it contains the potential for tremendously high evolution.

The personality is indestructible. The healthiest personality is a natural personality, unlike a political personality which is untruthful, or a religious personality which is artificially forged. Few politicians or religious leaders have a true personality because they are so twisted by their own pursuits that they become like trained actors. Few business people can be earnest in their business and still maintain their spiritual integrity.

To have a natural, everlasting personality, you must identify with the Way. The *Tao Teh Ching, Attaining Unlimited Life,* and *Stepping Stones for Spiritual Success* are books that can serve your natural, true personality and spiritual immortality, although they may not cater to your psychological whims like religions do.

An achieved soul has high intelligence. It contains *yang* spirits which remain together and have full capability. In an unachieved soul, the *yang* spirits are scattered, and only the *yin* sphere of the original life is left. Sometimes the ghost of an unachieved deceased person re-converges in an ethereal shape, but it has no capability.

Modern physics pertains only to physical matter or energy, which the ancients classified as *yin chi.* This, however, is not the impetus of the universe called *yang chi* or *yang* spirits, which I also call "responsive substance." I use the word substance, because *chi* or spirits are still a form of existence. Spirits, for instance, can make noise and can create light around themselves. They also have foreknowledge that does not depend upon circumstance.

In my book *Tao, the Subtle Universal Law*, I call the responsive substance the Subtle Law or the Way. Whatever you call it, it is the spiritual substance before it becomes personalized as great individuals. In a broad sense, there is no difference between a spirit and *chi*. In other words, *chi* and spirits have the same foundation, but *chi* is a broadly applied term that can also include "atmosphere." A spirit can have personality, or can at least be very responsive.

When spirits converge, they become a divine being. When they are independent, each of them is complete, with powers far beyond the scope of modern physics and its mechanical approach. They are also beyond the range of ordinary religions. They are the natural vitality or primal energy of the universe. As such, they can befriend and assist the incomplete knowledge of an achieved human individual.

The purpose of spiritual cultivation is not to become more attached to the physical form, but to attain the *yang* energy that animates life and nature. If modern physicists were ever to undertake spiritual self-cultivation, they would finally grasp the complete reality of nature and the universe.

All individuals are like actors or actresses. In the words of Shakespeare: "The world's a stage, and all the men and women merely players: they have their exits and their entrances; and one man in his time plays many parts..." (*As You Like It*). When people who have not cultivated themselves exit the stage, their personal energy scatters.

True immortality or everlasting life is the process of numerous responsive substances freely converging to become a soul or returning to a state of independence. This ancient discovery is much more valuable than any Nobel prize-winning discovery of our modern era. It is short-sighted to focus on the material foundation of life alone and neglect the natural foundation of the universe. A re-discovery of life is needed for all people today.

About 5,000 years ago, a new concept formed in the human mind. Some people assumed that there must be a powerful gardener who made the garden, a God who created the universe. Actually, it was an image that expressed a certain stage of human development. Mental growth is different from spiritual growth, which is typically much slower. For example, a person who grows spiritually and develops an integral knowledge of the subtle sphere cannot express his or her achievement well because it is not something that is easy to conceptualize or verbalize. Learning how to accurately express the truth takes time.

Religion often makes use of metaphors to express the inexpressible, but undeveloped people sometimes take these metaphors literally and create blockages to understanding the natural truth. Language can always be improved, but the substance or truth that is expressed always stays the same.

In modern times, it seems that religious conflict has escalated. People should examine the origins of any culture that obscures the universal truth. By making an effort to restore objectivity, people may be able to examine their religious beliefs impartially. This would certainly spare the rest of the world any further unnecessary suffering and bloodshed.

Chapter 9
The Subtle Response

The ancient Chinese experience was totally different from that of people of the Middle East and India who struggled harder for survival. That difference led to fundamental differences in development. The Chinese developed in a fertile region without having to compete for survival. Because the land was vast and ample, people were able to simply walk away from each other and relocate. This brought a kind of cooperative peace, which nurtured the development of such accomplishments as the *I Ching*.

The reason why the *I Ching* works is because of the existence of a subtle link between all people and all things through energy correspondence. This subtle energy connection is the spiritual nature of the physical world. God is but the spiritual response of nature.

The *I Ching* provided an objective view of the universe and was later elucidated in the *Tao Teh Ching* by Lao Tzu. The *Tao Teh Ching* is essentially derived from the *I Ching*.

During the last 50 years, the population of China has grown tremendously. In the generations before the Jing Dynasty (265-419 C.E.), the southern part of China was undeveloped and sparsely populated. People there had the chance to travel and experience the beauty of the land, and they wrote poems and songs about the earth. The beauty of the land sings beautifully through a resonant human mind, and the Way did not need to be searched for, because it was self-evident in the peaceful nature and peaceful lives of all people. The beauty of nature preaches the Universal Way in the eloquence of the sunlight, moonlight, murmuring rivers, whispering winds, blossoming flowers, singing birds, flourishing vegetation, and the great chorus of all lives saying "Holy, holy, holy."

All religions are deviations from nature. Tao exists among all races and tribes in the world, not just the Chinese.

Chapter 10
The Pursuit of All Natural Individuals

The USIW is a self-governed society. Its spiritual source is the ancient natural tradition whose original values can be respected and adjusted as your own direction in life.

I. Three Important Bonds
Respect your society and work to support its healthy condition.
Protect your children and guide them in a healthy direction.
Love your spouse and give him or her practical support.

II. Three Obediences
Follow the highest rationality.
Follow correct knowledge.
Follow good advice.

III. The Four Traits of My Being
My virtue.
My words.
My direction of life.
My manners.

IV. The Five Constancies of a Balanced Life
A kind heart
Wisdom
Righteousness
Faithfulness
Fitness

V. The Five Blessings
Good health
Financial freedom
Love of virtue
Longevity
Natural transformation and ascension

Chapter 11
Heaven is a Goal for Development

In most western religions, Heaven is the place where God reigns separate and apart from the world. The Heaven of Judaism, Christianity, and Islam is septate, meaning that it has seven parts that include the sun, the moon and the first five planets.

In India, Heaven is somewhat bigger. By including the constellations, it expands to 33 levels: 28 constellations, plus five planets. The sun is God, and the moon is his queen.

The Chinese recognize 36 Heavenly bodies: the 28 constellations plus the seven stars of the Big Dipper, which are seen as the hands of the big clock in the sky. Since of these seven stars is a double star, there are 36 rather than 35.

The Big Dipper is the center of the 24 climatic points in the yearly cycle, as well as the 28 lodges of the lunar cycle of each day in the lunar month. The concept of "center" brought forth the image of the Jade Emperor, the most exquisite and most refined spiritual reality of the universal mind.

The Three Pure Realms are a metaphor for the pure body, the pure mind and the pure soul. They are also used to describe the three divisions of the sky called the *San Ching*. The space from earth to the North Star is called *T'ai Ching* (Great Purity) and nurtures the natural vitality of life. The space surrounding and above the North Star, including the area visible to the naked eye and the galaxy itself, is called *Shan Ching* (the High Purity) and supports the development of the mind. The space further above the North Star to infinity is called *Yu Ching*, (the Supreme Purity) and supports the development of the soul.

The Three Pure Realms are not only actual locations, but are considered as spiritual expansion and attainment, internally and externally, both before and after the formation of life.

In a practical sense, the Three Pure Realms are the three spheres of the nature. They are the ancient spiritual view of nature as a spiritual sphere (Heaven), a material sphere (Earth) and a life sphere called People as the medium between Heaven and Earth. The unity of all three is called the Way or Tao.

All Heavens are limited and small compared to the vastness of the universe itself. Small, cozy Heavens are only psychological toys for a certain stage of human growth. Nevertheless, different numbers of Heavens became the foundation of many traditions, and have been passed down to modern descendants. If correctly understood, belief in these heavens was a small step toward a better individual life. Should we not readjust our vision to include the common benefit of all people? Heaven is never a cause for fighting, but a potential for rediscovering the natural unity of all people.

The teaching of the Integral Way promotes spiritual development. The amount of development you achieve and the level of knowledge you attain will determine which Heaven you live in. When you spiritually integrate and reunite the fragmented pieces of your being to function as a whole, God or Heaven becomes an achievable reality. The 28 constellations become 28 steps of the circulatory movement of the "Cosmic Tour." The 36 Heavens become the 36 steps of the Heavenly Ladder of artful spiritual learning. Each step opens up a new spiritual experience for developing one's soul and for reaching different spiritual dimensions which were called Heaven in ancient times. These steps are taken in order to fulfill one's own spiritual completion.

Chapter 12
Spiritual Reality is Not Far Off

God is a collective spiritual body whose focus is the benefit of all life. The human soul is also a collective body with at least 3 levels of energy: physical, mental and spiritual. Yet this obvious reality is still unrecognized by so-called advanced medicine in the most highly civilized countries of the modern world. Western medicine insists that life exists on the material level alone, without looking past the physical body at a person's whole life. Even when the spirit is gone, they prop up the body and expect to revive it mechanically later. When the spirits leave the body and that level of life is no longer active, there is no life any more, but doctors and hospitals offer no peace to a departing soul. Life has natural reasons for ending, and there is nothing that medicine can do about them.

What can be achieved is the art of maintaining spirits as colleagues of the body. Because spirits are invisible and unformed, most people don't understand their value. Although it is the most subtle level of universal or individual life, the soul is the most essential level of natural vitality. The natural environment needs to be respected so as to not damage its subtle vitality. An undistorted image of God is the healthy vitality of nature and individual lives.

The true expression of God is to live, to be true, to be fundamentally healthy, to be balanced, to be harmonious, and to be supportive of all life. God is life; it does not drive or push, it supports. When danger comes, God warns you, but you may not hear it if your mind is too busy or too impulsive. Even a fatal warning may not be noticed at a critical moment.

Religions that are mere mental projections can never reveal reality. God is the soul that connects the internal and external spheres of life; this important fact is lost in the teachings of most religions. Spiritual achievement is the only means to personal improvement and higher evolution.

Chapter 13
The Way Comes From
the Power of Normalcy

For the most part, folk Taoism is very similar to Hinduism and other religions that worship statues, walls and stones through sacrifices, offerings and prayers. Demonstrations such as walking over hot coals, climbing ladders of sharp knives, pushing nails through the palms, or using narrow swords to pierce their faces, etc. all mistake physical phenomena for the power of God. Actually, they are nothing but a kind of witchcraft.

The Universal Way restores one's relationship with nature and with oneself. Because we are one with nature, she does not discriminate among us by religion.

The ancient wise ones did not separate spiritual practice from their daily lives. The great service they offered to the people of their time was to realize the universal spirit in everyday life. No truly beneficial development can come from being unnatural.

Chapter 14
Losing the Way Changes a Government From Serviceable to Abusive

Fu Shi (dates unknown), Shen Nung (reign 3218-3078 B.C.E.), the Yellow Emperor (reign 2678-2598 B.C.E.), Emperor Chun Shui (reign 2510-2436 B.C.) who was the grandson of the Yellow Emperor and an ancestor of the branch of the Ni family, Emperor Gou (reign 2436-2366 B.C.), Emperor Niao (reign 2357-2255 B.C.), Shun (reign 2255-2207 B.C.) and Yu (reign 2205-2197 B.C.) were all teachers of the Universal Integral Way who served the world, unmotivated by personal interest or privilege. Their efforts helped keep society natural and healthy.

During the early period of Chinese society, an emperor or social leader was still required to meet high spiritual standards; they were moral symbols of selfless service. Because there were not many laws then, people followed an emperor's example in their own lives. If the emperor did not live by a spiritual standard, he was abolished by people.

The early emperors were "barefoot emperors" who received no payment or special privilege for their pure service. This is why they were respected as gods, because the ancient Chinese concept of God, or *Ti*, was the protective, helping power of Heaven. Since people had not seen a real god, they drew their image or understanding of God from these early selfless emperors, who were quite different from later land robbers and villains who called themselves emperor.

In his early middle age, the Yellow Emperor humbly requested instruction from the long-lived Kuan Chen Tzu, a great achieved one. The instruction he received was this:

> *The power of life that comes from nature is subtle.*
> *You can nurture it by keeping your life peaceful.*
> *When your mind is at peace,*
> > *all of your activities become natural.*

The way of eternal life is
    to not disturb the spirit by the mind,
    and to not exhaust the form
    (the body and nature) by fantasy.
Unite the spirit with the formless essence of nature.

This ancient teaching contains spiritual guidance of perpetual value.

The following piece was passed down directly from the ancient barefoot emperors through Niao (2357-2258 B.C.E.), Shun (2257-2208 B.C.E.), and Yu (2207-2197 B.C.E.).

The Universal Law is subtle.
Human desire is wild.
Unite yourself with the universal subtle law,
    and maintain your life
    in the most centered, creative way.

This message also has perpetual spiritual value.

The Chou Dynasty (1122-249 B.C.) was a time of virtue and moral strength, setting an example that held the whole society together. During the early Chou dynasty, there were more than 500 small kingdoms. Among them was the Ni family, who assisted in King Wu's revolution. The central government rewarded our family by recognizing us as the Ni kingdom, which is now Teng County in Shen Dong province. Previously, we were called Jee, meaning "a beautiful or charming girl," which was something that was admired and respected by the natural society of earlier times. This was the natural surname of the Yellow Emperor and of King Wen. Today people admire men's muscles, but the source of Taoism came before the time of masculine dominance over the world.

At that time, it was not that big a deal to be a king because there were so many of them. A small kingdom was only the size of a modern county. I believe my ancestor had 1,000 chariots, which is why it was called the State of a Thousand Chariots by the Chou Dynasty (1122-256 B.C.E.).

Until the Sung Dynasty (960-1279 A.D.), there were only about a hundred surnames in China, most of them related to the Yellow Emperor or Shen Nung. This is to say that the members of our family are not the only descendants of the Yellow Emperor. What is very worthwhile to mention is the humanistic culture founded by the Emperor that our family has continued. It was later collected as the Yellow Emperor's Internal Work, and we have valued it for generations.

By the end of the Chou Dynasty, people no longer respected the emperors, because they did not live up to recognized spiritual standards. This decline led to the Period of Spring and Autumn and the Warring Period (403-247 B.C.), during which the smaller kingdoms became stronger than the central government of the Chou Dynasty and the lords competed for military leadership. The Chin Dynasty (248-207 B.C.), was the winner of this competition, because its leader destroyed all the other kingdoms to establish a unified empire under his own control. That was how China received its name. This aggressive and brutal dynasty lasted for only two generations, a total of 40 years. I support cultural and political unification when it is accomplished peacefully and harmoniously, not when it is the result of cruel control that is cursed by generations of people.

Chapter 15
Bad History Repeats Itself

I

The wise ones who helped establish the Han Dynasty at the end of the Chin Dynasty (206 BC - 219 AD) were true Taoist sages. One of them, Old Sage Yellow Stone, ("The Precious Instruction of Old Sage Yellow Stone" is contained in the booklet *Progress Along the Way: Life, Service and Realization*) to whom the Yellow Emperor's and Lao Tzu's achievement had been passed, gave his esoteric teaching to Chahng Lang, the top adviser of the Han Dynasty.

Another achieved one who was active at the beginning of the Han Dynasty was a sage known as Ho Shan Gon, the "Respectable Old Man of the River." The esoteric teachings from the ancient development of Tao that were passed down through him are included in my work, *The Esoteric Tao Teh Ching*. At least a dozen of his students lived during the early Han Dynasty, when group activity by developed individuals first began to take place.

During this period, highly educated people began searching for their ancient heritage. Duke Liu Ang found his teachers, the Eight Achieved Ones, whose arts of *dao-in* I have put into practice as the Eight Treasures and *Dao-In*.

At the beginning of the Han Dynasty, nature was respected and the principle of *Wu Wei* or non-interference was followed. At that time, government was not a burden to people. When government becomes a burden, the organic nature and prosperity of a society is damaged. When a government sets the direction for a peaceful, orderly society, people prosper by themselves. This was the principle of the ancient natural sages.

Unfortunately, not all individuals of the Han Dynasty followed the Way. Dong Chung Shu (179-93 B.C.), a Confucian scholar, helped Emperor Wu (reign 140-36 B.C.) establish political control over China by taking a religious approach. Emperor Wu was a very ambitious young man who, with the help of this Confucian scholar, mixed political power with religious belief in order to unnaturally elevate his position as emperor. Although Wu Ti proclaimed himself the Son of Heaven, practically, he was still just an emperor. Since that time, the school of the Universal Way has retreated to rural areas, its students wishing to live ordinary lives and have nothing more to do with governments. Although we do not support any unnatural government, we are peaceful people. We do our spiritual practice and accommodate the changes in the world.

The bad example of the first Emperor of Chin, whose dynasty lasted so briefly in the long span of Chinese history, violated the subtle law by using too much violence. Then Emperor Wu combined religion and politics and created a sickness that deviated still further from the Way of a natural society.

Change is inevitable. In 1912 Dr. Sun Yat Sen's revolution tried to correct an unjust social system, but failed due to internal struggle and external invasion. When communism gained control of China, it taught the world a profound lesson in how the organic condition of a society and the natural course of life could be destroyed. The twentieth century in general has marked a change from the time when people were self-governed and natural society was orderly.

Good times can be brought about by a good leader or government, and bad times by a bad leader or government. Whoever has political power can create benefit or trouble for people. Religious control has a similar effect. People's conception of God is reflected in the condition of their lives and in the openness of their society.

When times are good, God is good, and when times are bad, God is bad. However, the truth is that good and bad times are brought about by people themselves. In other words, poor self-management and poor leadership are both sources of trouble. You cannot blame it on God, in the sense of an external influence that interferes in people's lives.

II

You may not be interested in knowing about Chinese history, and it is not my intention or interest to be a history teacher, but it is a seldom told story of human growth that you have a right to know.

At the beginning of the Han Dynasty, a school of philosophy based on the teachings of the Yellow Emperor and Lao Tzu was formed. The people of the Han Dynasty had just crawled out from the ashes of the Chin Dynasty and they truly understood the value of a normal, healthy society. They naturally formed a school of philosophy called the "School of Thought of the Yellow Emperor and Lao Tzu." You do not find such schools in good times when people have normal lives. However, when the world is troubled, people seek a different approach than the social or political marketplace. Then, with an unattached spirit, achieved ones such as the Old Fisherman, Lao Tzu, Yellowstone, Chahng Lang, and Ho Shan Gong (the Old Man of the River), fulfill their spiritual duty to society in a spirit of unattachment. They are creators of history, while other more famous leaders are created by history.

Chapter 16
The Trouble of the West
Is the Trouble of the East

The philosophical and scientific inspiration of Western culture comes from ancient Greece. In his dialogue, *The Republic,* Plato attempted to restore the teachings of his teacher Socrates. It is clear that both teacher and student applied human intelligence externally in order to shape society so that all individuals would fit into it.

The tendency of the mother can affect the tendency of the offspring, and the West has inherited a cultural disposition toward having a mastermind that makes external arrangements, regardless of whether that mind has reached maturity or not. This disposition paved the way from Socrates and Plato to Jean Jacques Rousseau (1712-1778), who wrote *The Social Contract,* and to Karl Marx (1818-1883), who wrote *Das Capital.* Later problematic developments all came from this early habit of designing other people's lives, thus the tendency toward governmental control of all aspects of people's lives became stronger and stronger. Two extreme examples of this are communism and Hitler's national socialism, both of which originate from the use of social force to arrange the world, the government and the people. Such interference in individual lives is an incomplete inheritance from the worthwhile cultural achievement of the Greeks.

Let us take a moment, however, to examine whether culture should take all the blame. When you read Aristotle's *Ethics* you can see that Aristotle, who was a student of Plato, corrected the tendency toward imposing a social plan on society. I feel that he sensed a more complete picture of life in which each person's ethics forms the foundation of the society.

Politicians and leaders today should not forsake the healing lessons of Aristotle's *Ethics*. In modern times, national policies use external force to hold people together and heavy taxes or social programs are established to make people dependent on the government. This trend is not too different from a dictatorship, except that political parties share the booty. Such policies create problems rather than undo them.

A healthy society cannot be idealistically arranged by the minds of its leaders. It should only be guarded from negative tendencies. Parents should guide their children in the same way. To allow for each child's natural growth and development, parents should not twist a child's natural tendencies. Good social plans cannot be produced by twisted or immature minds. One of the worst problems of the human world is intellectual sickness, especially that of leaders and politicians who treat the world as their victim.

Aristotle's division of knowledge into various subjects of science is the foundation of modern western development. However, his philosophy and ethics were not accepted by the West. This one-sided trend has brought material expansion to the western world, but it has also left it spiritually less developed than many countries that are economically and politically less developed. Material life is external, which is suitable for making practical arrangements. Spiritual life is internal. As life becomes more focused on what is external, the internal essence of life becomes hollow. The spiritual qualities of freedom, dignity and independence are not subject to external forces. Thus, a society must be built on respect for the individual rather than on social control. Control damages human nature and its positive virtues, one of which is personal initiative.

The American Revolution established a model of government that respects the natural rights of the individual, private enterprise, and political independence. But today, that hard won individual self-responsibility is threatened by policies that lure people backwards into dependency on the government, baiting them into a new form of slavery.

Aristotle's ethics and the ethics of individual spiritual cultivation are related, but they are not totally the same, because the great philosopher's spiritual knowledge was incomplete. However, unless each person works to refine the ethics of his or her own life, politics and social life have no root and will become unbalanced. The essence of ethics is respect for virtue. Without virtue, no social program has any positive meaning, and no intellectual achievement can serve life correctly; they will only become destructive to the naturalness of human nature. This is the result of partial or one-sided development.

We can witness what masterminds have done to the world. In the second century, when Constantine's royal scribes edited the life and teachings of Jesus, the New Testament was revised in a way that distorted the peaceful image of Jesus and his real teaching, thus turning Christianity into a dogmatic social system that has suffocated the naturalness of western society for the last eighteen centuries.

Few people were or are aware that there are more recorded teachings of Jesus than are contained in the New Testament. In the twentieth century the Dead Sea Scrolls revealed that Jesus belonged to a particular sect of Judaism. He was a normal spiritual teacher, not a melodramatic figure who preached an other-worldly kingdom. Most interesting of all, there is no mention of a crucifixion!

Constantine's scribes chose to portray Jesus' death as similar to the death of Socrates, with the negative implication that virtuous people are always persecuted. The Catholic Church adopted Greek philosophy and established new rituals to create a religion that would rule people's souls with shackles and chains for centuries to come.

Long afterwards, the Protestant movement, led by Martin Luther (1483-1546), attempted to make Christianity more reasonable. Since that time, many spiritual leaders have seen through the veil of social religion and have revised the style of worship and re-elucidated the New Testament.

The human spirit, like other aspects of life, is part of the overall progress of universal life. If it does not continue to grow, it will become a source of trouble. In modern times, intellectual development has advanced more rapidly than spiritual understanding, resulting in much evil, in both the East and West. The worst mistake of the West has been for people to give up their own spiritual efforts by trusting churches, and for intellectuals to not have anything to do with churches. This has kept religion at the level of mythology and has led to the divorce of religion and science, which breeds very poor cultural leadership. Meanwhile, the talent of the Constantinian scribes has been passed down to modern screenwriters in Hollywood, where anything is possible.

Jesus' teaching aside, he was totally reinvented as a person who sacrificed himself to save the world. This implies that good people, if recognized, must be sacrificed by society; that is negative idea. The teaching of salvation, redemption and the last judgement reinforce the cult of self-sacrifice. There is no value at all in an inhumane culture. None.

The core trouble comes from turning spiritual life into contracted, compulsory social behavior. Old or new, covenant means contract. Covenants turn spiritual life into a form of commerce: negotiating how much God will do and how much you will pay. The ancient Jews set very precise terms on the relationship between God and people. This is one part of the cultural influence that has externalized western life to such a great degree and caused people to overlook the internal essence of life.

The material success and social control of western culture has lead to internal failure. Without internal essence, we live lives that are shallow and hollow. When the relationship with God is contracted, the relationship between loved ones, such as parents and children, husband and wife, etc., become contracted obligations as well, and there is no essence to life. Heartfelt love is gone with the west wind.

A life is true when its internal essence finds a suitable means of expression. That is a spiritual achievement. Life should pursue happiness, but happiness does not come from contracted behavior. Love, which is the essence of human nature, is also not contracted behavior.

Social programs that do not disrespect individual effort cause true human dignity to die. When democracy descends into partisanship, the openness and benevolence of a free society dies. When external worship is overexpanded, the spirit dies. With too many procedures, the effect of work or ceremony is damaged. With too much ritual and formality, the meaning of an event is lost.

I like the West; I live in the West. However, I also see the trouble that comes from western cultural leadership. Although they choose to worship Jesus, people should worship his anti-hypocrisy rather than the myth that he died for their sins. How could Jesus die for you? Such a story only produces a negative belief in the righteousness of suffering and persecution, creating a gulf of darkness and ignorance between people and God. It suggests that you should allow the negative elements of your life to destroy your positive life energy.

When weapons are so strong and the spirit is so dwarfed, there is the danger of imbalance and unnaturalness. Lao Tzu warned long ago that when a small child brandishes a big axe, it can seldom avoid hurting itself.

Why not replace old, narrow attitudes with the Universal Way? It is well received by people of universal conscience everywhere, although their numbers are small compared to the rest of the world's population. I welcome you to join me and help society find a healthy spiritual direction. Personally, I support the USIW as a society of students, teachers, workers and supporters of the College of Tao and the Universal Way.

The Universal Way reunites all parts of life without discarding any valuable spiritual experiences of the past. A healthy spiritual life is not exclusive to one tribe or one race, one era or another, it represents a stage of human development. Spiritual progress is an awakening. A complete life unites all parts of life through past experience.

Chapter 17
Spiritual Foundation Above Religion

Shamanism, or spirit worship, is not an organized religion. It is generally found in primitive cultures and does not develop into a social force. Religions, on the other hand, are social organizations that use set beliefs and rituals to unite people for worldly purposes.

There are some people who are devoted to universal spirituality rather than to one religion in particular. To be devout in that sense means that you are very focused and earnest with respect to universal spiritual reality. That is different than being devoutly religious.

Everything in the universe is part of one great life. In trying to explain and illustrate this ancient teaching to modern people, I have written many books. I wish that all people of spiritual attainment would teach other people by following the ancient example of selfless spiritual service that asks nothing in return. The original goal of the Universal Integral Way is to serve the spiritual growth of all human beings. If the world is well guided, that purpose will be achieved.

Traditional Chinese medicine was a service that developed from the immortal pursuit of individuals who hardly ever engaged in social activities. Among them were Kou Hong, Dou Hong Jing (both of whom served in politics, but with selfless motives), Sun Shih Miao, Ssi Men Chung Ching, and many others.

Sometimes it is hard to distinguish between truly achieved ones and religious idols. For example, among the popular Eight Immortals in China, none were involved in establishing a religion. They were masters who cultivated and achieved themselves, and later they became figures of religious worship, just like movie stars who cannot stop people from forming fan clubs.

It is not our concern how people view us. Our main task is to work together to benefit the everyday people of the world so that they can continue to develop spiritually.

I have been teaching and writing about Tao for decades, however the truth is not a word. The subtle truth that is embodied within us is not limited to one way, one form, one language or one symbol, but it is all ways, all forms, all languages and all symbols. In order to enjoy spiritual freedom, the human mind must break down all walls and doors that block the simple essence of unity. The Universal Way leads us to step out and meet all people in one divine eternal light of the wordless subtle truth without denying the great variety of human customs.

Chapter 18
The Useful Heritage

I

Most people do not appreciate the value of simplicity. When their emotions become too fanciful, they look for something untruthful to fill their simple, truthful lives. For the most part, personal beliefs are only fantasies rather than anything related to reality.

Religions often sell fantasies in place of the plain truth of life. The Universal Way simply presents the everyday truth of everyday people. No one can live without it. It is the "bottom line." All wonders, mysteries and fantasies are contained in one's own natural simple life, and naturalness is invaluable to spiritual life as well as to physical life.

I have described some of the valuable prehistoric contributions of the ancient achieved ones. These spiritual arts were first gathered by the Yellow Emperor on his visits to mountains and rural places to pay homage to the great achieved individuals of his time.

A second collection was made at the end of the Chou Dynasty, when society started to fall into chaos. In the early Han Dynasty, those who respected natural spiritual attainment put great effort into recording these teachings in book form. One such individual was Hui Nang Tzu. The essential spiritual practice of the Universal Way is the collection that was made during the Golden Era of China, from 722 to 359 B.C. Most of these practices, however, remained esoteric.

II

The Chin Dynasty unified China into one large society through military force. Unification can facilitate many aspects of life such as communication and transportation, but the price of tyranny is high. Excessive control by a central government damages the health of a society, just as having a congested head causes a stroke.

Any society, big or small, needs good bi-directional communication both within the government and between government and the people. Neither side should give all the orders or set all the rules, because that would be one-way communication. The ancient developed ones compared the running of a society to the life of an individual. Circulation to all organs and limbs must be complete in order to prevent imbalance and sickness.

In the following guidance, Bao Tzu, one of the founders of Zahn (Zen) Buddhism, advised Emperor Wu Ti of Liang (reign 502-549 C.E.) against neglecting his social duties and devoting himself to the fantasy of Buddhism:

People do not understand the Way.
Thus, they wish to remove the vexation of maya.
The maya of the mind has no reality.
You are on the way of life
    that you are searching for.

When you are aware of your conscious being,
    that awareness is the
    spiritual substance of self.
You do not need to look for it.
The great truth of life is right in front of you.
People confuse themselves
    by looking for something
    to replace their own self-nature.

The self-nature of life is pure.
There is no need to adorn it.
There are three Lords
    that command people's lives:
    greed, anger and ignorance.
No struggle has any use at all.

It is only the absurd insistence of people
*   that creates trouble for themselves and others.*
It is not too late to awaken to reality.
It is not too soon to give up the mess.
There is no difference
between Buddha and people.
There is no difference
between great wisdom and foolishness.
Each person has their own bright pearl.
There is no need to search for treasure elsewhere.
The true and the false have one source.
The awakened and the worldly are on the same path.
There is no difference between experiencing nirvana
*   and experiencing life and death.*
All of these are conditions you hold onto.
At the time you expect enlightenment,
*   when you manage to quiet down your mind,*
*   you create a fuss and fussiness instead.*

There is only the Way of no way,
*   which is the true way.*
From the way of nothing,
*   comes all things.*
When you embrace nothing,
*   you attain wholeness.*

This was not only an important teaching of its time, but
it also has become spiritual guidance of perpetual value.

The Tang Dynasty, whose hallmark was openness, was
a great time in Chinese history, somewhat like the United
States is today. It adopted the policy of accepting all
cultures, and this led to a new social integration that took
place during the Sung Dynasty, when many imminent
individuals devoted themselves to reviewing, absorbing and

preserving the treasures of those cultures. At this time, I would like to give you four tenets of that period:

1. Realize the Heavenly Way in your own life. Realize that the natural order of your daily life is the same as the order that is within you.

2. Eliminate all unnatural personal desires.

3. Follow your innate sense of good and bad. Respect your own sense of being pleased by beauty and being displeased by bad odors. Such functions are instinctual. To recognize good and bad is also instinctual. Conform to what is good and do away with what is bad.

4. Objectively research all useful knowledge.

Among these four guidelines, the people of the Sung Dynasty did not practice the fourth one enough. Also, the second one was sometimes misinterpreted to mean all desires, even those which are healthy.

The spiritual direction of the Ming Dynasty (1368-1644 C.E.) was a continuation of the Sung Dynasty in that people still tended to be spiritual rather than practical. They did not put energy into the fourth tenet: "Objectively research all useful knowledge." The Sung Dynasty was a time that exalted erotic pleasure and all types of luxury, which led to internal corruption and external invasion.

During the Ching Dynasty (1644-1911 C.E.), the government did not support further cultural development. Some developed individuals awakened to the need for practical research of useful knowledge in order to improve the life condition of all people, but politicians of the time had no long-term view, and thus did not support it.

Then China met with the drastic changes of this century. The Republic of China (1912) was founded under Dr. Sun Yat Sen. Later, the communists copied an extreme model of government from Russia. Now, they have moved away from treating collective labor like a concentration camp and have begun to recognize the value of a free market, and even the value of the individual, to some degree.

The Universal Way remembers the lessons of the past, so it serves people selflessly. We do not focus on one religion or tradition. Our spiritual practice is non-partial. We respect non-ideological spiritual unity and simplicity. We are open to the light of wisdom. In a balanced way, we digest and absorb the spiritual guidance of the ancient developed ones and find the Heavenly Way by developing an orderly world within ourselves.

The Universal Way eliminates unnatural personal desire and respects instinctual knowledge of right and wrong. It objectively researches all useful knowledge, recognizes the value of all cultures, and puts past ideologies behind. It eliminates cultural separation and works toward a better individual life, family life, and social life for all people.

I teach spiritual achievement instead of religious practices, but some individuals still think that not having a religion is like having no home. The teaching of universal integral truth does have a religious level that offers truthful service without the immature and imbalanced tendencies of conventional religion. The integral truth not only teaches essential spiritual practices, it also provides practical spiritual beliefs that can be applied to all aspects of life.

The Universal Way holds the spiritual foundation of a natural and balanced life. It is also:

the foundation of spiritual self-responsibility
the foundation of a spiritually dutiful life

the foundation of universal unity
the foundation of the most centered, creative spiritual life
the foundation of universal harmony
the foundation of universal essence
the foundation of encompassing all useful variety
the foundation of a creative and virtuous life
the foundation of universal spiritual care
the foundation of universal benefit
the foundation that is open to progress
the foundation of spiritual wholism
the foundation of no dogma or meaningless rituals
the foundation that recognizes all healthy knowledge
the foundation of self-cultivation and refinement
the foundation of smooth relationships
the foundation of not forsaking a decent worldly life
the foundation of respect for universal spiritual value
the foundation of cultural and spiritual filtration
the foundation of bowing to universal beauty,
    goodness and truth

A teaching, or an individual person, could not have that many names, but each name carries many important meanings. It is simpler to just call it the Universal Way or the Integral Way. My goal as a teacher is to uplift the spiritual condition of the whole world by promoting the three spheres of health in all people: mind, body and soul.

Chapter 19
The Ageless Teaching
of Long and Happy Life

I

The ageless teaching of long and happy life is the hidden treasure of humankind. In modern times, the world looks up to scientific achievement. In ancient times, exceptional individuals pursued special spiritual achievement through actual practices rather than through social activities focused around a temple or monastery or church. Those teachings were, and still are, beyond the public domain. Just as all people do not need to know how to make an atomic bomb, certain practices have also been kept secret in order to protect them from being misused.

Special practices can enable individuals to develop in gradual stages. In ancient times, each stage was called a Heaven, but in actuality it was simply the maximized experience of a scope of life that lay beyond the ordinary. These practices were scientifically arranged so that progress could occur safely, by degrees. There was also, however, a certain level of adventure at the same time.

Modern science only knows the physical surface of life. It does not know that life and the world consist of small lives that I call sensible energy. I have said previously that life is composed of many tiny spiritual entities and that this can be proven by doing certain practices. This is not to be taken on blind faith. Such things are not for the public, but for those who aspire to attain the natural truth.

Physical life is three dimensional, but when you examine life deeply, you realize that mental life and spiritual life also have multiple dimensions. Some are safe, others are not; but how do you know unless you experience them? The ancient attainment was to maximize the experience of life with safe guidance and learning. This level produces no material gain, so it does not interest the majority.

It is not suitable for all people to face the difficulty of being a student of immortality. Some students, however, should continue the ancient development in order to prevent it from being lost. The high teaching should be taught in the traditional way without being confused with general religions or conventional schools of thought. High attainment has always been a serious matter, and the requirements are not simple. Obtaining an opportunity for such learning does not depend upon the grace of God, but on individual subjective effort. The teacher chooses the student. At the same time, each individual needs to fulfill his or her self-discipline, moral obligation and duty to society. Virtuous fulfillment to society, which is also known as good deeds, is required.

The ancient culture should remain a hidden treasure of humankind. Few people even know of the existence of these arts that offer an individual proof of what I have written about in my books. The indestructible spiritual reality of life can be your own attainment.

My publications can help most people to achieve a long and happy life. They don't need to search for anything other than deepening their learning with that as their foundation.

II
The Traditional Approach of the Immortal School

Recently someone asked me: "I think that truth is something real that we must live, not something to merely know or consider, not just an idealistic concept that can be intellectually debated. What is the truth of how to live well during all stages of life, including old age and even up to death?" This is a question of great concern to many people, and I need to reply accordingly.

Life is not only a matter of consuming food, having sex and making money. Those things limit the scope of life to the physical or bodily level. In modern times, science

presents life only on the surface level of anatomy, bio-
chemistry, neurology, and the intellectual level of psychol-
ogy, thus modern people tend to become overdependent
on the material sphere of life and will often exchange their
lives for unnecessary things. This is a different direction
than that of a balanced natural life.

Most people know that life has three main spheres:
body, mind and soul. Those three spheres of natural energy
comprise a unit. However, the ancient natural development
with its effective practices found many different dimensions
of life. In other words, development is derived from the
practices, and the really good practices enable you to
experience many dimensions. Achievement is a matter of
finding the most effective practice and endowing it with
your personal effort.

At the time of the Warring Period toward the end of the
Chou Dynasty (starting in 403 B.C.E.), the most active
individuals, aside from competing kingdoms, were a group
called the People of Special Formulas. When the small
feudal kingdoms were actively competing to replace the
declining Chou Dynasty, the People of Special Formulas
were concerned about the general culture and about preserving the ancient spiritual arts. Many spiritual achievements were saved but then lost again. Some have survived
and are still available. These practices are the legacy of
people with strong spiritual ambition who were determined to develop and broaden their life experience.

72 spiritual arts were chosen from the 3,600 spiritual
methods and practices that were collected. These 72 arts
can be divided into two categories: foundational arts and
esoteric (or specific) arts. Each category has 36 arts which
are for deep development. Each of these 36 categories has
12 levels for each of the three spheres of life, with specific
practices for developing the body, mind and soul.

Have you read that Lei Tzu traveled by riding on the
wind? That was one attainment; in modern times, it is called

levitation. Chuang Tzu did not think it was a high art, however. In his opinion, the highest art was to rely on nothing. Nevertheless, these 72 arts are preserved and continued by the School of Internal Harmony. The ancient developed ones acknowledged that one's physical life is supported by one's family and society, but a long and happy life depends upon oneself.

The first 36 arts have been discussed and taught in my previous publications. They include Traditional Chinese Medicine, acupuncture, herbology, *feng shui*, etc. Although *feng shui* has become a questionable practice, its original value was to create harmony for the individual or family, and to choose the location where they would live. It was useful knowledge; however, it has become twisted by psychological applications.

Practices for specific purposes have not yet been made public. These are the practices that verify what I teach; they are for those who not only like eating the fruit but also enjoy growing the trees. Life is deeper than a modern person thinks it is. Many healthy and enjoyable experiences are possible in a life that is complete.

When small, children are cared for by their parents, but when they are teenagers, their sense of independence starts to grow. Typically, however, spiritual interest begins only when a person is troubled or experiences a troublesome time of life, when there is difficulty, struggle, threat of danger. Such things make people turn inward, thus spiritual interest grows. People's search starts when they cannot see their future.

Spiritual learning can bring spiritual development. As a lifetime interest, spiritual self-cultivation can go hand in hand with worldly life. If you are really interested in developing yourself spiritually, you can do so regardless of your age, although it takes years to become really proficient at the arts of body, mind and spirit. These arts can be an important part of your life; then you can still go deeper to learn the highest development. You may not necessarily use practices beyond those of the fundamental level, but you can work on the more essential learning. This takes many years, so all in all, you could spend your whole lifetime in the discovery of the depth and enjoyment of life.

All people are obligated to develop their lives, otherwise they become their own or someone else's burden. However, few taste the spiritual fruit that comes from doing effective practices that are available to purposeful people.

In ancient times, if you were lucky enough to find a real teacher, you had to be tested before that teacher accepted you and taught you the arts. No schools were open to teach such high development, no advertisements would tell you that you could learn this. You might have a chance to learn one or two of those arts from a teacher. Each year or so, when you went to pay homage to the teacher, the teacher would look at your situation, and he might teach you something. This is how the ancient immortal teaching was given.

However, he also might just give you some advice or even say nothing at all. The energy you present is read by the teacher. The teacher knew how to read you and how to guide you or to leave you alone.

Through individual teaching, you learn. The teacher determines what you receive according to his knowledge of your possibility for development. What you learn is not something for you to sell, but for your own self-development.

The spiritual education of ancient times was not a religious teaching. You meet the developed one, and the teaching was individual to individual, done in a free style rather than like the relationship between a business and its customers. It was not given to the masses, it was a special opportunity for students who aspired to develop themselves above the pursuit of food, sex and financial freedom. The immortal learning added greatly to their lives; they had great fulfillment with no stress, because their focus was not worldly intention or contention. Their purpose in life was not to serve God or serve life, but to develop a life above that.

Otherwise, people are born into the world and live a short while, with their attention pulled away by the hectic society around them. They don't know where they came from nor where they will go; they only experience their physical being. In such a life, there is no great achievement other than academic degrees or epitaphs carved on tombstones.

In the past 2,000 years, different schools have developed under the guidance of different teachers. Only some parts of the whole practice were emphasized. Among the earlier schools, the school of Shuan Ching was an improvement and revision of the earlier Heavenly Teacher school; the school of Ching Ming (pure brightness) was the ancient sun worship, which can be linked with middle eastern practices; and the renewed immortal school of the Tang Dynasty (618-906 B.C.E.) brought the ancient practice of spiritual immortality forth again. The Thunder School of the Sung Dynasty (965-1279 B.C.E.) further strengthened the ancient practices.

I would also like to mention two other sects if the ancient teaching of Tao that found an avenue of survival through Buddhism. One is Chan or Zen Buddhism, which maintained the teaching of Lao Tzu and Chuang Tzu. The other is the original Red Sect of Tibetan Buddhism which combined and preserved Buddhist doctrines, Hindu rituals and Taoist practices. The Taoist practices were originally connected to the sun, moon and stars, but were revised to personify Boddhisattvas in the new religion.

In other sects of Tibetan Buddhism, meditation skills included the visualization of images ranging from demons to Buddha's palm print, but the essential meditation of visualizing bright spots in the body came from the star practice of Taoism and Hinduism. Tibetan Buddhism also recognized a very basic system of energy channels in the body, such as rising, sinking, parallel and winding *chi*.

The Red Sect has preserved some of the ancient secret practices such as the way of death, which can be a natural phenomenon that releases bodily particles as part of the process of leaving the physical world. Tibetan lamas and nuns would spend their entire lifetimes preparing for the moment of their death, however this contributed to a certain pessimistic influence on the Buddhist view of life.

In general, Chinese culture has always been a melting pot. Buddhism, Islam, Zoroastrianism, Manichaeism, Confucianism and Taoism exist side by side and were, for the most part, absorbed into Folk Taoism during and since the Sung Dynasty. Each tradition has been able to make its unique contribution to Chinese culture, thanks to the ancient humanism that prevailed for countless generations, but while religious warfare never found a foothold in the broadly humanistic culture of China, political mania did. Communism brought wholesale slaughter to China on the basis of ideological beliefs that disguised raw greed and ambition. If China's population were the size of Rwanda's, no one would have survived the calamity, but China happened to be large enough to withstand the losses of millions upon millions of innocent people.

Good thoughts, good customs and good philosophies are of service to people and are important to society, but they are of secondary importance because they are only conceptualizations of good *chi*. The ancient achieved ones understood that human life is guided by the mind, but they also understood that the mind is connected with light, natural light which is transformed and condensed. The mind is actually able to store light, and this internal supply of light energy is the course of what we call consciousness. It is like the energy link between telephones and computers.

Many ancient people worshiped the sun, because life on earth is closely connected with the sun. However, ancient Egyptian, Incan or Mayan sun worship or modern day sunbathers who lie on the beach like a bunch of dried sardines do not practice the ancient Taoist way of nurturing light internally. Nor do they address the kind of light that is released by the fusion of a sperm and an egg.

When the Yellow Emperor consulted the sages Guang Ching Tzu and Tien Chuang Huang Ren, they were already over 1,000 years old. How did they live that long? I can tell you without requiring you to kow tow. They knew how to assimilate light.

Master Lu, his teacher Chung Li Chuan and his friend Chen Tuan ate nothing and drank only a little wine each day to help their circulation. Lao Tzu lived to be over 200 years old, and the secret he shared with the world was: "I appreciate having eaten from my mother." In Chinese, the word for mother is made of two words: sun and moon, with star in the middle. (母) In the immortal tradition, the term *yang* refers to sun energy, while *yin* refers to moon energy. The esoteric practice of internal alchemy, called *rei tan* (丹), means the combination of the sun and moon. The names of different masters of the Immortal School contains further clues. Master Lu's spiritual name, Chung Yang, means pure *yang*. His student Tzu Yang's name means purple *yang*. Master Zan Chu Yang passed his knowledge to students who also adopted the word *yang* as part of their spiritual name.

Wise students learn to value their natural vitality and nurture it by using natural resources and approaches. If you are conservative by nature, you simply don't do anything that would harm yourself or others. If you are creative by nature, you do good things for yourself and other people. These two simple guidelines contain the essence of any useful religion.

Immature people are attracted to superficial religions. Mature people look for the essence behind all rituals and ceremonies, although rituals and ceremonies help young people form good habits that shape their internal reality. The Integral Way, which takes the essence of life as its foundation, serves the world at all levels, not just the level of social custom. Its true purpose is your spiritual achievement, although it can only show you the way.

Immortal cultivation brings true sublimation of personality. The broadness and depth you reach depends upon your own development. Not all virtuous individuals develop their wisdom. Not all people of high intelligence live life to its full depth and breadth.

I was motivated by the trouble of the world, and I made a vow to teach. This is what kept me doing the same thing year after year. Yet, through my own experience, learning is not a matter of social honor, it is for attaining the secret of spiritual immortality and realistically achieving oneself. Traditionally, the opportunity to learn is only given to the right individuals who are seriously undertaking spiritual sublimation and personal refinement.

Most people in the world are a mixture of good and evil. There are plenty of evil leaders who are supported by foolish people; together, they cause the downfall of humanity by focusing on social expansion and stirring up contention.

Needless to say, they do not encourage people to improve themselves. Political systems and religions have both become systems for cheating people and have not offered any great service for the past 2,000 years. This situation will continue until people stop pursuing short-term benefits and engage in their own development instead. As each person works for their own self-development, there will eventually be hope for a change in the world. Otherwise, mistakes and tragedies will continue to occur generation after generation. There must also be comparatively wiser leaders who will develop themselves instead of luring people into one pitfall after another.

III

An aspiring student may pursue advanced classes on the level of life *chi* training. Those with a special interest in the Self-Reliance Health Program, health, self-healing, and complete development can learn all of these separately. Each art or skill has its own value. When all comes together, it is one piece. This is what the Integral Way means.

Level I: The Level of T'ai Ching (The Sublime Body)

Life *chi* training includes actual skills used by oneself, including the high levels of *chi kung* and other methods. These skills will aid participants in their own cultivation and good health. There are 12 sublevels of independent practices.

Level II: The Level of Shan Ching (The Sublime Mind)

These skills will help the individual focus on spiritual empowerment and self-government toward continuing in his or her effectiveness and avoiding "burn-out." Level II will include learning a cultivation that will unite the practitioner with the Big Dipper and the North Star. There are 12 sublevels of independent practices.

Level III: The Level of Yu Ching (The Sublime Soul)
High spiritual development is attainable. These are specific practices taught by Master Ni for the exclusive use of the most advanced spiritual students, and are never to be taught to anyone whose spiritual quality does not meet the learning. There are 12 sublevels of independent practices.

Each of these three levels has twelve sublevels, totaling 36 steps, in a spiral that spans the height and depth of self-development. Traditionally, at least one training session was taught per year to impart the training of those arts. They were always taught on a individual basis. It was said, "Never is the teaching given where there are six ears," meaning that only two individuals could be present, the teacher and the student. The teaching was only given when the teacher intuitively determined that there were participants who were prepared to accept and use it appropriately. I feel I need to make an adjustment for modern students to learn in the collective way for some levels. Traditional principles are still respected by giving the small, less formal classes, yet individual instruction and having close contact between the teacher and student is still the most important learning process. Traditional discipline and restrictions are chosen and adopted. It depends upon how much enlightenment the mind of the student has reached. Sometimes less important ones should be lifted during small, less formal classes, but individual instruction is still the most important learning. It is the teacher's spiritual response directly to the student through the flesh form. Even with the same teacher, the responding spiritual divine one could be different.

IV

You may not need to learn everything, but you may like to know the sketch of the whole. Now I would like to offer you the ancient way of learning and training, which can be part and can be whole.

The foundational level, which I have presented in the West for the past 20 years, was mostly developed by special individuals after Lao Tzu, i.e. after around 500 B.C.E. To the general public, those arts and practices hold the potential for deep exploration and attainment. They are rooted in ancient achievements and have been experienced, tested and proven to be sound by many generations. Some people value and preserve them, but not for the purpose of social promotion.

What was taught before the time of Lao Tzu was different from the publications I have given on the foundational level. Those practices are less artistic, but they still touch on the central essence of life. For the last 8,000 years, people have used the sun and moon as a symbol for *yin* and *yang*. Earlier people accepted the North Star as the center of all heavenly bodies, because it appeared that all stars rotated around it as the center. Some heavenly bodies are above the North Star, some beneath it, and some surround it. The North Star and the Great Wolf Star take turns being the axis of the northern night sky, with the Big Dipper as the arm that points out the direction of seasonal and monthly differences. The earth aligns its axis with the North Star for 100,000 years, then with the Great Wolf for 100,000 years. Ancient people used that alternation as a symbol of *yin* and *yang*.

The *T'ai Ching* level or the level of self-reliance falls in the scope of the North Star. Immortality is limited to the sense of time in the range beneath the North Star. The spiritual attunement achieved through this training gives one the ability to surpass physical limitations.

The *Shang Ching* level or the level of self-sufficiency is closer to the energy surrounding or in the neighborhood of the North Star. This is a higher immortal level. The spiritual attunement from this training is the ability to surpass the mind's limitations.

The *Yu Ching* level or the level of self-completion involves achievement beyond the scope of the North Star. The practical goal of spiritual attainment from this training is to surpass the limitations of soul.

V

The educational system of the ancient developed ones is interesting. They were fully aware that human emotional force is very unreasonable, and that many capable individuals who could manage the world are unable to manage themselves.

People need constructive activity to keep them healthy. Stagnation makes a person sick, like murky water that stays in one spot. Every year, learning something new can refresh your life energy. It is a practical way to refresh your life.

To be a teacher is to vow to accept one's duty. A mature individual is less happy being with immature individuals. However, that is the state of the world. To be a student is to be happy. Some people are very happy because they find growth each year through the process of learning. Some of them choose to be teachers to share their attainment with worthy individuals while at the same time, they continue to be lifetime students. This was how ancient knowledge was passed along. This way of passing knowledge was like a "pony express." One individual passes the information or skill to the second one, and the next and the next.

Some teachers do not make it easy for you to learn, because privacy is the prime asset of their spiritual lives and they do not like to be disturbed. You need to mobilize your intention, sincerity, virtue and deep mind to learn anything from them. You might be tested and tested before being accepted.

The long and happy lives of people in ancient spiritual communities were accomplished by their useful and meaningful way of learning and teaching, achieving and forgetting. Students were not required to learn from them or to know all the practices. Learning the ancient arts was a privilege, a lifetime opportunity, a useful pursuit and a challenge. Some students learned one or two arts, were satisfied and enjoyed what they learned for their entire lifetime. Some took decades to learn one thing well and then would go back to learn something new. Some were like the flowing water of a pure clear stream, singing the song of a happy life full of interesting experiences from spiritual learning. These generations of learning are not like the stiff lineage of religions. The process of learning and teaching resembles the long Heavenly River above, which you call the Milky Way.

VI

According to Lao Tzu's own experience, he said, "Learn only a little. If you learn too much, you become confused. Each time, each year, you learn only one thing. This is the principle of good learning."

You may accept all of these practices as the conscious expansion of the ancient natural mind. Learning them will eventually develop your sense of life. In my tradition, the ancient developed people and teachers stayed in mountains or rural places. Once a year, every three years, or every nine years, students came to learn from them. Those who came back many times, up to 36 trips, learned all the levels and sublevels, to secure their achievement. As I see it, the purpose was to constantly refresh their lives.

One might learn all 36 levels, for it takes at least 36 years
to really learn those arts. On the high level, the teaching can
be a few words, which is above the level of art. If you learn
one art each year, and keep practicing it for the whole year
to reach real achievement, you won't have time to compete
with the world. You only have time to compete with
yourself, which means to improve your state of well-being.
By doing these practices, you change yourself from being
on a heavy physical level to having a light energy body,
from the stubborn mental level to be the flexible universal
mind, and from the ego-centered level of life, you uplift
yourself to the universal soul. There is a need for practical
achievement in accomplishing self-completion or upliftment,
because you are formed by the world physically, mentally
and spiritually.

After you have become achieved, start to review what
you have learned during the past for another 36 years. Then
start to re-review all you have learned for another 36 year
cycle. You continue until you drop your old "physical
clothes." Useful activities are what make you interested in
a long life. This is ancient wisdom and natural inspiration
rather than intentional design. The achieved ones had no
interest whatever in worldly attractions.

The number of learning cycles you can complete depends upon the age at which the opportunity to learn
comes to you. In general, not until late in life do most
people become aware of the value of their life. Few young
ones ever think about such things. If you start learning a
complete 36 year cycle during late middle age, for example
at age 65, your spiritual pursuit will result in an unconscious
increase in your will to live. Thus, you will probably
lengthen your age from one to several 36-year cycles. Some
ancient achieved people lived a very long time. Lao Tzu,
for example, lived for more than 200 years, Pan Tzu lived

up to 800 years, and there were many others like him whose names were not recorded. However, legends and folk stories of those immortals are abundant.

As I view it, this learning makes you a more respectful and valuable person in your old age. The traditional culture honored and respected elders; the longer one lived, the more respect was given because the individual was wiser. Today's commercial culture is different.

Because this type of cyclic renewal trains or patterns the soul, achieved ones repeated this cosmic tour with their achieved soul, using the North Star as the center of the cycle. The 360 degrees are interpreted as 36 years. They kept rotating around this immortal path; this is where the concept of immortality comes from. I recommend that when you have a chance to learn this type of cosmic tour, you do so. The possibility of immortality comes about through uniting with nature, not separating from it. The constancy of nature is expressed by all the stars as they circle around the North Star in the center. The North Star itself circles another center, and so on.

This profound learning can uplift you from the earthly level to the celestial. You do not always need to struggle here. Your future is far ahead. The term "Cosmic Tour" does not mean the *T'ai Chi* exercise by that name, although the exercise can be an illustration of it. The immortal path is the 9 x 36-year cycle, as the minimum standard for refining your soul.

VII

Different practices stimulate the brain and body differently, thus keeping them fresh and enduring so that the individual can live longer physically, although an achieved soul survives physical death and continues cycling in the sky.

In the cyclical training, first you learn from the teacher, then you become self-trained. By so doing, you stabilize your spiritual essence with rotation and cyclic movement by following the North Star. Once you are in space, you have immediately broken the year of 364 1/4 days. The length of time is decided by the distance above the earth.

I mentioned the teachings that were developed before the time of Lao Tzu or even before the time of the Yellow Emperor almost 5,000 years ago, that were continued by Lao Tzu. People who live in general society should concentrate on working on the foundational levels and forget the teaching that came before Lao Tzu or the Yellow Emperor.

The esoteric level of teaching should be maintained as esoteric and should not be revealed to others on a whim to avoid a wrong choice or confusion with worldly religions which mostly conflict with the true teaching of Tao. If you are in the service of sick people, you may give some of it to them, but the whole picture is only known by the complete training. The esoteric teaching is not a matter of merely giving or receiving information, it is a matter of totally plunging your life into the universal energy. You need to prove and verify everything that the teacher teaches you by your own attainment. The essence of the ancient esoteric teaching comes from a totally different culture than the socially centered culture of the last 2,000 years. Ancient society focused on individual natural life and respected its relationship to nature. Modern society has no such focus.

Since I have fulfilled the teaching given to the general public, my further intention is to teach the ancient achievement to a few individuals who want to break free from everyday coping with the modern world. This teaching also helps people stay focused upon living a natural life rather than worldly pursuits that carry such heavy internal and external pressures. In other words, you can learn how to dilute the influence of and be unengaged with the human world while still living in it. You can develop your range of life to extend beyond the limits of modern culture. I don't know who will be interested in accepting the universal order of cyclic movement and use it to shape the spiritual constancy inside themselves instead of following external authorities. If social competition is no longer your business, you may find yourself to be a real winner.

The requirements of a student of such learning are high. I do not know who shall persevere with great spirit through all 36 years of learning, then review it for another 36 year cycle, then continue with a third and a fourth cycle, etc. Those individuals must have a mind that is not scattered by the external attractions and excitement of the modern world. When you are achieved, you have the freedom to jump out of the natural flow of life at any time or not at all.

The immortal world makes no discrimination of time or space. There is no birth limitation, as there is in the world; you no longer struggle with such things. You become an unnoticeable immortal who lives in the ordinary world of undevelopment and turmoil. I am interested in forming the Immortal Club by teaching a few individuals who have the type of mental capacity that can enjoy timeless, spaceless, self-generating cyclic practices.

Chuang Tzu once said, you shouldn't bother to talk about ice and snow to insects who only live in the length of summer, but I do not encourage anyone who is not ready to commit themselves to a lifetime of learning in the school that travels around the 36 Heavens.

Living among the 36 dimensions will make you feel different. Your life will be like one of those Heavens. My deep reflection is that it obviously reverts the aging process and makes you like a child again, forever youthful, spiritually.

I have mentioned that Tao is the way. The Way to follow is the way of nature. Nature is formed by all types of cycles, the most impressive being the cycle centered by the North Star, which makes all life tick. Lao Tzu's *Tao Teh Ching* is the introduction to such esoteric practices. Without such practices, nobody could achieve anything.

My work and teaching seems to serve people for much longer than they can conceive of. Those who do not have such a deep interest should continue learning the fundamental levels that are found in my publications and videos. The foundational level comes from the depth of my own training. Even on that level, I have revealed some of the esoteric teachings in order to help those who need them.

The Treasure Map of Immortality

Chapter 20
Two Important Invocations

The Invocation of Seven Stars
The system of the seven stars and the North Star
*   in the northern sky*
*   are the piloting light for my soul in its universal tour*
*   and for all lives on earth.*

Heavenly divinities roam above it.
Mount Kun Lun is far beneath it.
From it, the universal order can be observed.
From it, Chyan *(Heaven) and* Kun *(Earth) are attuned.*
It is the point around which all heavenly bodies rotate.

Although the highest divinity is beyond form,
*   its subtle purple light constantly strengthens me*
*   in my worldly spiritual mission.*
My life is empowered by the response of the Jade Emperor,
*   the Universal Divine One,*
*   the Universal Divine Energy.*

Prayer to the True Lord of the Universe
Among all things,
*   none are my Lord,*
The only true Lord is
*   the universal conscience*
*   that safeguards the peace, harmony and prosperity*
*   of all people.*
A balanced mind and a universal heart
*   are the messengers of the true Lord.*
Among all things,
*   none are my Lord.*
The boundless light of my sublime soul
*   is the only true Lord.*

Chapter 21
The Symbols of
the Shrine of Universal Light

At the Yo San University of Traditional Chinese Medicine in Santa Monica, California, we have set up a shrine for yearly spiritual renewal services in which certain symbols are used. In our Shrine of Universal Light, above the altar there are three pictures that symbolize the Three Realms of High Purity. These are the mystical spheres of life, with the spiritual sphere at the top. The structure of the altar, which represents the levels of actual spiritual attainment, is designed to help support our lives. It also symbolizes the completeness of life that the *Tao Teh Ching* elucidates:

Tao gives birth to one.
One gives birth to two,
   and the gives birth to three.
Three gives birth
   to all things and beings.

Integralness of Tao:

One (yang)

Two (yin)   Three
                        (integration of yin & yang)

The Natural Trinity of the Universal Way

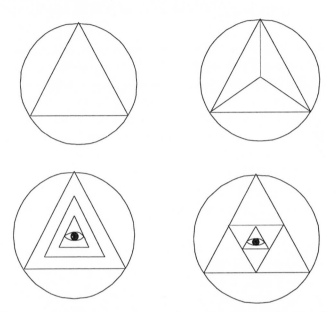

All four diagrams express the Tao that gives birth to one. One gives birth to two, two gives birth to three and three gives birth to the myriad things that all express the integration and interdependence of universal relationship and the universal truth of oneness. Each of these diagrams has a specific meaning that expresses life and the mysterious sphere of nature.

The next two diagrams represent the integration of *yin* and *yang*.

Since the dawn of natural culture, the ancient developed ones recognized that there are three spheres in the universe:

    a. the spiritual sphere or sphere of Heaven
    b. the material sphere or sphere of Earth
    c. the life sphere of sphere of Human Life

Together they are called the Trine of the Universe and Individual Life that composes all of nature.

There are three kinds of fitness:

Fitness of soul

Fitness of mind   Fitness of body

There are three bodily energy fields for dynamic spiritual cultivation:

Upper

Middle   Lower

These three bodily energy fields are called the *tan tien.*

There are three divinities:

Heaven

Earth   Humankind

The common term for all useful, balanced trines is interpreted as the Three Peaces or the *San Ching* which means the peaceful way of body, mind and soul. The three highest mysterious universal realms are:

Supreme Peace (*Yu Ching*)

Middle (*Sang Ching*)   Lower (*Tai Ching*)

In each human life, there is a body, mind and spirit that express the Trine of Life and should not be separated from one another or from the rest of nature.

At the mental level, the trine includes your intelligence, your passion and your will.

At the social level, the trine includes your character, your capability and your health.

At the spiritual level, the trine is composed of the Upper, Middle and Lower Soul. The Upper Soul is the spiritual sphere of the individual. The Middle Soul is the authority of the mind. The Lower Soul is the authority of physical desire.

When the three souls harmonize, the individual is at peace; thus, internal unity is the source of stability in an individual.

The 36 Arts of Full Development of Universal Life

The outer octagon is *tai ching*, the middle octagon is *san ching* and the center octagon is *yu ching*. Together, they are the complete development of the cosmic person.

When you are quiet, you discover a dialogue going on in your mind or brain. It is not hard to notice the conversation that is taking place because there is always a quiet listener when such dialogue happens. Among the three souls that rule your life, each consists of a group of tiny invisible spiritual entities that represent one of the spheres of your life. These entities are the inherent spiritual function and vitality of life.

Accordingly, the ancient developed ones said that life is like a kaleidoscope and that when the images of one's life turn upside down "one should not be confused by the new design." It is merely a phenomenal expression of the subtle reality behind it.

A perfect personality contains three powers: universal love, wisdom, and the courage to carry out the wisdom and universal love.

In the Shrine of Universal Light, the yellow robed being represents universal love. The green robed being (sometimes blue or blue-purple) represents wisdom, and the red-robed being represents the courage or warmth of life.

You may wonder why the three beings are all men. *Yang* energy is usually apparent, while *yin* energy is usually hidden. All beings have some part which is apparent, some part which is hidden. Men and women are thus equal, but men are used as symbols of the expressible level of life.

Because each individual represents a unity of *yin* and *yang*, the symbol of *San Ching* was adopted by Kou Hong of the Jing Dynasty (265-419 C.E.). (Please read *Life and Teaching of Two Immortals: Volume I, Kou Hong.*) In his shrine on Lufo Mountain of Canton Province in China, where Kou Hong cultivated himself, I think these images must have been more simple than the paintings in our shrine.

We do not practice idol worship, but we do use some symbols to remind ourselves of how to correctly fulfill our lives. The space of the shrine is a multi-level classroom, and the pictures on the altar are symbols of our own lives.

Before Kou Hong, shrines and altars were not indoors but were placed in natural settings that could be shared by all. Of course, different times use different symbols, but their meaning is the same. There is an important poem expressing universal oneness:

The three wonders of the sky
*   are the sun, moon and stars.*
The three wonders of the earth
*   are water, fire and wind.*
The three wonders of my life being
*   are ching, chi and sen*
*   (reproductive energy, vitality*
*   and spiritual energy).*
All wonders are integrated in my life being.

In the old tradition, the philosophy of the universe as one life was firmly established in people's everyday perception of internal and external, individual and society, etc. One ancient symbol of universal oneness was the cauldron.

After food was cooked, it was offered to the sky and to the natural surroundings before being distributed to the families attending the meal or ceremony. This expressed the viewpoint that all people are brothers and sisters. Sometimes wine would be poured into a small cup and offered to the sky and the natural surroundings before being sprinkled over the ground, again expressing the intention of sharing the blessing with all lives.

In the Shrine of Universal Light, there are pictures of my father and mother, who set such examples in their generation of living with the Three Purities: clean body, clear mind and peaceful soul. I obtained their photos 40 years after I left China. The pictures were restored from the ruins of the so-called cultural revolution that happened in the 1960's when many people in China became extremely ideological.

The Shrine of Universal Light is usually open for the yearly spiritual renewal ceremony so that people can experience these symbols and review their hidden meaning for use in their own lives. No temple, sanctuary or shrine, however, is more magnificent than the altar of your own life being and bodily life. This is the direct manifestation of universal nature. At the heart of your life is the altar of the Shrine of the Eternal Breath of Tao.

Chapter 22
The Completeness of Life

Spiritual learning is not same as the brutal faith of social religions and undeveloped people. The fact is that human spirituality is a delicate matter. Most religions are dogmatic and lack flexible instruction. Some modern societies do not respect rationality, but foster extreme religious fundamentalism. This does not help the world or themselves.

The spiritual teaching of the Universal Integral Way takes a delicate approach that supports your physical, emotional and spiritual health so that you can have a creative and productive life. It particularly guides your intellect toward benefitting all people and all lives.

Spiritual learning can only be taught to people who have a delicate quality of mind. Through systematic and methodic training, they can rediscover themselves and find the true foundation of life, in a scientific sense. Modern sciences, such as genetics, have still not discovered the key to the door of life. I truly wish to pass such knowledge on, because I know it can benefit modern values about things such as health, money, morality, lifestyle etc.

Human culture is an interesting phenomenon. You have the freedom to teach all kinds of junk, but when there is something truly valuable, it needs to be protected from the majority. Spiritually achieved teachers have traditionally disguised the truth in symbolic language. Those who initiated new religions were usually achieved, but they were not necessarily the ones who wrote their teachings down, thus truth and falsehood developed at the same time. The false may have been developed to protect the truth, or it could have simply been a different level of service.

A proverb in my tradition says that there are 36,000 practices, and all teachers insist that theirs is the truthful one. Some spiritually responsible teachers filtered the 36,000 practices down to only 3,600 practices, but this was still far too many.

Generations of highly developed spiritual individuals not only worked to maintain their own essence, but also reached out to learn other peoples' achievements. They filtered the 36,000 practices down to 3,600, then to 360, then to 108. Because each practice usually requires at least one year to become familiar with and benefit from, you would need to spend 108 years as a student. So, they were further distilled to 81 essential practices, but that was still too many, so the 81 were reduced to 72. Out of those 72, 36 of the most direct and precise practices were selected. Those 36 practices were divided into three levels, each containing twelve sublevels. Each sublevel contains one important practice, which I have mostly presented in my publications. However, if you know how to respect universal unity and live a natural life, you can ignore all practices at all levels.

So the 3 levels containing 36 practices actually covers 72 important practices, which contain the essence of 81 practices. The 81 practices contain 360 practices, which contain 3600 practices, which cover the broad scope of 36,000 practices in all.

Because people are all at different stages of growth and because life has so many different aspects, there needs to be a wide choice of suitable practices to help people develop themselves.

In ancient times, after people had developed spiritually, they worked on a simple subject like how to make a wheel or how to pile differently shaped stones into a wall. Good achievement is connected with both intellectual and spiritual strength. Daily work should be respected, because it stimulates the brain to develop. The brain assists the hands in creating. The brain is still the tool of the highly developed spirits.

Intellectual knowledge is not the root, it is only the leaves and branches. Modern people write a lot of books, but in ancient times there were no big publishing houses, so knowledge was passed down orally. It carried a sense of mystery, particularly the early knowledge of chemistry, which seemed magical. In the West, chemistry was called alchemy, and then witchcraft when the church gained control of society.

In a natural society, however, problems are often solved methodically. Once in a mountain village there was a man who was spiritually achieved. Many visitors heard about him and came to seek his guidance, and they usually asked the same question: "What is Tao?" The man usually raised one finger or just a thumb and said nothing. People accepted this respectfully and left.

The achieved one had a student who stayed with him. This student thought, "That is easy. I don't need to stay too long to learn that." So one day, when the teacher had gone on a short trip, someone came to visit and asked, "Is your teacher home?" The student simply said, "What is your question? What are you looking for?" The person asked, "What is Tao?" The student proudly raised his finger in answer. The man came up to him and held his finger down with his hand and asked again, "Now tell me, what is Tao?" The young student said, "You are holding my finger. How can I tell you now?" The visitor said, "Demonstrate the Tao to me without using your finger." The student said, "I haven't learned that yet."

I ask you, can you exhibit the integral truth without using your finger? I was such a student when I was young. I attained my direct experience at the age of 43. Soon afterward, I found that it only serves myself and no one else. Then I worked to personally verify the existence of spirits and life through a specific practice, because that can reveal the truth of universal energy to update modern medicine, the new science and other important, related aspects of life. I achieved it. If anyone uses my method, they can achieve the same result. Since my late middle age, I have dedicated myself to improving the spiritual condition of the world.

Chapter 23
Conclusion

To me, the most important thing to accomplish is the rediscovery of life. If you don't understand the foundation of life, you will only see the formed part of life and will never know the assistance that can come from the unformed part of life. The unformed part of life comes from the formed part of life. How does the formed part of life produce the unformed spiritual function? This is not a problem of the question being difficult, but of being lazy and not learning the truth of natural spiritual reality. Once you learn it, you don't need patented religions or narrow scientific theories. You will know the value of life and the meaning of death. You will know how much support you should give to the government and society and how much you should work for yourself. Should you choose patriotism? Should you choose the affectionate or passionate object of your love as a cause for life or death? Should you work harder or work less? Should you listen to your labor union or should you listen to yourself? You can find these answers by your own discovery. Without self-discovery, it is hard to say that you are really the one who lives your own life.

Here, I have retouched a poem given by a friend to conclude the support of spiritual unity among all friends:

Attach to None of the Bits and Pieces of People,
But Find the Unity Among Them All

People important to you,
    people unimportant to you,
    all pass through your life.
Touch them lightly with your love
    and move on.

When some people leave you,
    you breathe a sign of relief
    and wonder why you ever
    came in contact with them.

When other people leave you,
    you wonder why they had to go away
    and leave such a gaping hole.

Children leave parents,
    friends leave friends,
    acquaintances move on.
People change homes,
    people grow apart.
Enemies hate and move on.
Friends love and move on.

You reflect on the many who have
    moved into your hazy memory.
You look on those present
    and wonder.

I believe in the starry energy
    of the "Weaving Maid" in the sky,
    weaving the world with connections between people.
The master designer moves people in and out
    of each other's lives
    according to the subtle law of correspondence.[1]
Each leaves his mark on the other.

You find you are made up
    of bits and pieces

---

[1] For more information on the Subtle Law, please read *Tao, the Subtle Universal Law, Key to Good Fortune,* and *The Natural Course of Spiritual Life: the Law of Causality.*

of all who have touched your life.
You are more because of it.

You would be less
      if they had not touched you.

Follow the Way of Infinity,
      and accept the bits and pieces
      in humility and wonder.
Never question and never regret
      the bits and pieces.
Bits and pieces fill the whole.

I am the universe;
      I am the Integral Way.
Bits and pieces pass away,
      but the Universe and the Way
      always stay.
This is how you live the Universal Way
      of Integral Life.

Attachment to None of the Bits and Pieces of Life

Things important to you,
      things unimportant to you
      all pass through your life,
      touching it with attention and non-attachment
      and moving on.

There are things that depart from you,
      and you breathe a sigh of relief
      and wonder why you ever came in contact with them.

There are things that depart from you,
      and you wonder why they had to go away
      and leave such a gaping hole.

Affection, love and friendship move on.
Things change and things grow apart.
Hatred moves on.
Love moves on.

You think about the morning
        on which love moved into your hazy memory.
You look upon those present and wonder.

I believe in the master of the subtle sphere,
        which is as the supreme law.
It moves things in and out of each person's life
        according to the subtle law of correspondence.
Each leaves its mark on the other.
You find life is made up
        of bits and pieces of things.
All have touched your life
        and you are more because of it.
You would be less
        if they had not touched you.

From the Way of Infinity
        you accept the bits and pieces
        without losing your own integrity and unity.
In humility and wonder,
        never question or regret or become impatient
        with bits and pieces.
I am the universe;
        I am the Integral Way.
Bits and pieces pass away,
        but the Universe and the Way
        always stay.
All fills the whole.
This is how you conduct
        the Universal Way of Integral Life.

Afterword

The practical level of learning Tao is very simple. Here I would like to recommend some sources that I feel are tried and true. Trustworthy guidance for all aspects of life can be found in the *Tao Teh Ching*, which is based on the ancient knowledge of nature that is expressed in *The Book of Changes and the Unchanging Truth* (the *I Ching*). If you are in doubt over what to do in a specific situation, *The Book of Changes* can provide insight and objectivity. If you are more interested in philosophical development, you can turn to Chuang Tzu, whose work I have elucidated in my book called *Attaining Unlimited Life*. Or if you prefer to explore the spiritual connections between people and nature, my book *Tao, the Subtle Universal Law* can help you. If you are looking for effective spiritual practices, the *Workbook for Spiritual Development* is invaluable. If you wish to learn gentle movement exercises such as Eight Treasures or *Dao-In* to improve your health and strengthen your spirit, there are videotapes to help you do so. If you want to practice meditation, the most effective way is described in a book called *The Golden Flower*, which was translated from the Chinese by Richard Wilhelm, with a commentary by Carl Jung. I have incorporated its teachings in various publications such as *Quest of Soul, Gate to Infinity,* and *Spring Thunder: Awaken Your Spirit With Dynamic Meditation.*

These books can become the mainsprings of your spiritual life. In them I have described many spiritual arts without trying to confuse or discourage you by the profundity and vastness of the Integral Way. Whether you ever read a spiritual book or are able to learn directly from a teacher, you are still a complete life being who can develop yourself by living a quiet, normal life and practicing subtle observation. This is a great achievement, although most people never notice it. It is beyond the judgement of people and God. It is how the culture of Tao originally developed. You live as the universe, because you are the universe.

Some people feel that they cannot achieve this without guidance, thus I offer my publications and teachings of the Integral Way. I also offer a Correspondence Course and occasional seminars (please see the form in the back pages of request further information). However, please remember that no truth is higher than the truth of your own life correctly lived.

A good life is a collection of healthy activities. Most cultures are designed to pull your energy out so that it will serve the society or the designs of special interest groups. People sacrifice their lives in this way without ever knowing why. Learning the Integral Way will bring your energy back to you. Its methods of self-cultivation teach you how to keep a balance between the centrifugal and centripetal forces in life. With balance, there is well being, and with well being you can contribute to peace and harmony in the world.

Selected books by Hua-Ching Ni

New Publications:
Gate to Infinity
Concourse of All Spiritual Paths
Natural Living and the Universal Way - VHS Videotape
Movement Arts for Emotional Health - VHS Videotape

Practical Living
Harmony: the Art of Life
Moonlight in the Dark Night
Golden Message
Key to Good Fortune
Mystical Universal Mother

Fundamental Readings
Stepping Stones for Spiritual Success
The Gentle Path of Spiritual Progress
Ageless Counsel for Modern Life
The Time is Now

Spiritual Classics
The Book of Changes and the Unchanging Truth
The Complete Works of Lao Tzu
Esoteric Tao Teh Ching
The Taoist Inner View of the Universe
Tao, the Subtle Universal Law
Workbook for Spiritual Development

Health and Exercise
Power of Natural Healing
Attune Your Body with Dao-In
Mastering Chi: Strength Through Movement

Esoteric Teachings
The Way, the Truth and the Light
Life and Teaching of Two Immortals, Volumes I and II
The Story of Two Kingdoms
Internal Alchemy: The Natural Way to Immortality
Mysticism: Empowering the Spirit Within

Selected Other Materials Available
from SevenStar Communications
on Natural Healing Arts and Sciences include:

Books
The Tao of Nutrition by Dr. Maoshing Ni
Chinese Vegetarian Delights by Lily Chuang
Chinese Herbology Made Easy by Dr. Maoshing Ni
Crane Style Chi Gong by Dr. Daoshing Ni
101 Vegetarian Delights by Lily Chuang and Cathy McNease
The Yellow Emperor's Classic of Medicine by Dr. Maoshing Ni

Pocket Booklets
Guide to Your Total Well-Being By Hua-Ching Ni
Progress Along the Way By Hua-Ching Ni
The Light of All Stars by Hua-Ching Ni
Less Stress, More Happiness
Integral Nutrition

Videotapes (VHS)
Attune Your Body with Dao-In by Hua-Ching Ni
T'ai Chi Chuan: An Appreciation by Hua-Ching Ni
Crane Style Chi Gong by Dr. Daoshing Ni
Self-Healing Chi Gong by Dr. Maoshing Ni
Eight Treasures by Dr. Maoshing Ni
T'ai Chi Chuan I & II by Dr. Maoshing Ni

Audiotapes (by Dr. Maoshing Ni)
Invocations: Health, Longevity & Healing a Broken Heart
Chi Gong for Stress Release
Chi Gong for Pain Management

SEVEN STAR
COMMUNICATIONS

If you wish to receive a copy of the latest SevenStar Communications catalog of books, booklets, videos and cassettes on alternative health topics, spiritual realization and movement arts, and to be placed on our mailing list, please call us at 310-576-1901, fill out this page and fax it to 310-917-2267 or mail it to:

SevenStar Communications
1314 Second Street
Santa Monica, CA 90401 USA

(Please Print)

Name————————————————————————————

Address————————————————————————————

City, State, Zip————————————————————————

Country————————————————————————————